Frillio's Pizza
Desktop Publishing Simulation

ISBN 0-9721331-3-5

Michael Gecawich

Published by
Business Education Publishing
Box 8558
Warwick, RI 02888
U.S.A.

For more information, visit our Web site at www.teachbused.com or
www.businesseducationpublishing.com

Copyright

Frillio's Pizza Desktop Publishing Simulation
Published by Business Education Publishing™
in partnership with Clipart.com™

Author
Michael J. Gecawich

Editors
Kathleen Cooney
Monica Handy
Diane Silvia
Linda Viveiros
Lisa Wardle

Student Reviewer
Peter Serra

Permissions
For permission to use materials from this text or the Frillio's Pizza Web site,
please contact us by:
Tel: 888-781-6921
Fax: 401-781-7608
Web: www.teachbused.com or www.businesseducationpublishing.com

Business Education Publishing
P.O. Box 8558 • Warwick, RI 02888 • U.S.A.

Adobe PageMaker®, Adobe InDesign®, Quark®, Microsoft Publisher® and Clipart.com® are registered trademarks of their
respective companies.

In the text and on the Frillio's Pizza Web site, any reference made to Frillio's Pizza and Joe Frillio is purely fictional and does
not depict an actual business establishment or real person.

Preface

Welcome to Frillio's (Free-lee-o's) Pizza: A real-world business simulation for desktop publishing and graphic design students

This simulation has been developed to provide desktop publishing and graphic design students an in-depth, real-world experience in developing business documents using desktop publishing software.

Frillio's Pizza Desktop Publishing Simulation contains a collection of eighteen documents that simulate those that would be needed by a real pizza restaurant.

Frillio's Pizza creates a scenario where you take on the role of a desktop publisher for the owner of Frillio's Pizza, Joe Frillio, who is about to open his doors to the public for business. By taking on the role of Joe Frillio's real desktop publisher, you will complete a comprehensive project that encompasses fun, strategy, and creativity.

Frillio's Pizza Desktop Publishing Simulation will challenge your design and page layout skills by presenting a wide variety of desktop publishing documents to complete. From designing a menu to creating promotional punch cards, you will get real-world practice and reinforcement in:

- Page layout and design
- Creativity and imagination
- Technical writing
- Critical thinking
- Establishing a real-world business identity
- Advertising and marketing
- Planning and decision-making
- Completing a real-world comprehensive project

Use this book in conjunction with your teacher's guidance and the use of desktop publishing software. The material presented in Frillio's Pizza is generic and can be completed using any desktop publishing software such as Adobe PageMaker®, Adobe InDesign®, Quark®, or Microsoft Publisher®.

It is assumed that you already have a basic working knowledge of at least one desktop publishing software application. This book does not include step-by-step instructions that differentiate between different desktop publishing software applications.

If you are using Microsoft Word® as your primary design software, you may have to slightly modify some of the page setup requirements in order to complete certain portions of the simulation.

So roll up your sleeves, and get ready to take on the document design challenges that lie ahead in Frillio's Pizza!

Contents

Introduction 1
    Welcome to Frillio's (Free-lee-o's) Pizza! 2
    A Message from the Owner of Frillio's Pizza, Joe Frillio 4
    Background Information About Frillio's Pizza 5

Using this Book and the Frillio's Pizza Web Site 7
    Understanding Each Part of the Simulation 8
    Using the Frillio's Pizza Web Site 10

Tips and Guidelines for Designing Great Documents 13
    Desktop Publishing Design Tips and Guidelines 14
    Make Your Content Come Alive! 21

Time to Get Warmed Up 23
    Warm-up Exercise #1: Pizza Brainstorming 24
    Warm-up Exercise #2: Pizza Restaurant Fonts, Graphics, and Headlines 25

Individual Parts of the Simulation
    Part 1: Design or Download the Frillio's Pizza Logo 27
    Part 2: Design the Frillio's Pizza Stationery 31
        2A: Design the Frillio's Pizza Letterhead 32
        2B: Design the Frillio's Pizza Envelope 34
        2C: Design Joe Frillio's Business Card 36
    Part 3: Design the Frillio's Pizza Place Mat 39
    Part 4: Design a Coupon Flyer 43
    Part 5: Design the Frillio's Pizza Menu 47
    Part 6: Create the Grand Opening Advertisement 55
    Part 7: Design a Refrigerator Magnet 59
    Part 8: Design the Frillio's Pizza Takeout Menu Brochure 63
    Part 9: Create a Bumper Sticker 69
    Part 10: Create an Hours of Operation Sign 73
    Part 11: Create a "Pizza Club" Promotional Punch Card 77
    Part 12: Create a Cup Coaster 81
    Part 13: Create a Gift Certificate 85
    Part 14: Frillio's Pizza T-shirt Design on a Flyer 89
    Bonus #1: Create a Poster 93
    Bonus #2: Create a T-shirt Raffle Entry Form 97
    Bonus #3: Create an Employment Application Form 101
    Conclusion: Download the "Job Complete" Title Page 105

Introduction

- Welcome to Frillio's Pizza
- A message from the owner of Frillio's Pizza, Joe Frillio
- Background information about Frillio's Pizza

Welcome to
Frillio's (Free-lee-o's) Pizza!

THE STORY OF JOE FRILLIO AND FRILLIO'S PIZZA

A long time ago in a small town tucked away in the pillars of Italy, a young boy named Joe Frillio had a dream. Joe Frillio dreamed that he would one day move to America and open one of the finest pizzeria restaurants. He would name his restaurant *Frillio's Pizza*.

Joe is grown up now and has recently moved to the United States to a town called Saucy, which is located in the heart of California. Joe Frillio is closer than ever to achieving his dream of opening his own pizzeria. In fact, Joe has found the perfect location for his pizzeria, and the construction phase is complete.

Joe Frillio is anxious to open his doors for business as he looks proudly at the sign that reads "Frillio's Pizza—Opening Soon." As people pass by the pizzeria, Joe envisions them as customers who he hopes will soon be dining in his restaurant.

However, before Joe Frillio can officially declare Frillio's Pizza "open for business," he has one last task to complete. That's where you come in. You see, although Mr. Frillio is an expert at cooking tasty pizzas, he knows very little about computer technology. Joe Frillio needs someone with exceptional desktop publishing skills to create, design, and print a wide variety of restaurant-related documents before Frillio's Pizza can be declared officially "open for business."

YOUR ROLE AS THE DESKTOP PUBLISHER

Throughout this simulation, you will take on the role of Mr. Frillio's personal desktop publisher. Don't worry. Mr. Frillio has been diligent in providing you with step-by-step guidance and instructions for producing each of the documents he needs. He has even hired a team of professional Web designers to put together a special Frillio's Pizza Web site (www.frilliospizza.com) to provide you with a host of tools to assist you in the production and design of each document. (*More about the Frillio's Pizza Web site later.*)

THE CHALLENGES THAT LIE AHEAD

Using a desktop publishing software application and your creativity and design skills, you will be challenged to create well-organized, attractive, and professional documents that Joe Frillio will use to conduct his day-to-day business operations at Frillio's Pizza.

The following is a list of the skills you'll be drawing on throughout the simulation:

- Page layout and design
- Working with graphic images, objects, and elements used in graphic design
- Creativity and imagination
- Technical writing
- Critical thinking
- Establishing a real-world business identity
- Advertising and marketing
- Planning and decision-making
- The willingness and determination to complete a comprehensive real-world project

WHAT YOU'LL BE ASKED TO DESIGN

Below is a complete list of the documents Joe Frillio wants you to create and design. Based on your teacher's instructions, you may be asked to create all or only some of the documents listed.

A List of the Documents That You Will Be Designing:	
Part 1:	Download or create the Frillio's Pizza logo
Part 2A:	Letterhead
Part 2B:	Envelope
Part 2C:	Business Card
Part 3:	Place Mat
Part 4:	Coupon Flyer
Part 5:	Menu
Part 6:	Grand Opening Print Advertisement
Part 7:	Refrigerator Magnet
Part 8:	Takeout Menu Brochure
Part 9:	Bumper Sticker
Part 10:	Hours of Operation Sign
Part 11:	Promotional Punch Card
Part 12:	Cup Coaster
Part 13:	Gift Certificate
Part 14:	Frillio's Pizza T-shirt Design on a Flyer
Bonus #1:	Poster
Bonus #2:	T-Shirt Raffle Entry Form
Bonus #3:	Employment Application Form
Conclusion:	Download "Job Complete" Title Page

Now that you know what documents you'll be creating, let's meet Joe Frillio.

A Message from the Owner of Frillio's Pizza, Joe Frillio

Dear Desktop Publishing/Graphic Design Student,

It is my pleasure to welcome you to the Frillio's Pizza Desktop Publishing Simulation.

As you have already been told, my expertise is in creating extraordinary pizzas. As far as desktop publishing and graphic design skills, I fall a bit short (no pun intended). That's why I need your help.

As my hired desktop publisher, you will be creating a wide variety of documents that are needed in order for me to officially open the doors of Frillio's Pizza. From designing my restaurant menu to creating promotional punch cards, your page layout, creativity, and design skills will be challenged throughout this simulation.

As you draw on your desktop publishing skills, pay careful attention to what you have learned. When customers begin pouring into Frillio's Pizza, I want them to get a sense of good spirit, a friendly atmosphere, and experience good-tasting, high-quality food.

I have carefully presented each task for you to complete in a neat and organized manner. In addition to this book, I have hired the services of a Web design company to create a special Web site (www.frilliospizza.com) to assist you in the development of each document.

So roll up your sleeves, and get ready to cook up some creative desktop publishing documents as you embark on the Frillio's Pizza Desktop Publishing Simulation.

Let's get cooking!

Sincerely,

Joe Frillio

Joe Frillio
Pizza-Maker Extraordinaire and Owner of Frillio's Pizza

Background Information
About Frillio's Pizza

Good desktop publishers and graphic designers know their client. Throughout this simulation, you will be asked to include specific details and information about Frillio's Pizza. The following information will help you to become familiar with the restaurant.

Frillio's Pizza Contact and Background Information:

Company Name:	Frillio's Pizza
Description of the Business:	A family-style pizzeria restaurant offering customers a place to enjoy fine-cooked food served inside the establishment, for takeout, or for delivery.
Company Slogan:	"The best pizzeria in town"
Established:	When you complete the simulation
Address:	111 Pepperoni Drive Saucy, CA 92888
Toll-free Phone Number:	1-888-FRILLIO
Fax Number:	1-888-654-7814
E-mail Address:	Owner@FrilliosPizza.com
Web Site Address:	http://www.frilliospizza.com
Hours of Operation:	Mon - Thurs 11 am - 9 pm Fri, Sat, & Sun 11 am - 10 pm
Mission Statement:	To provide a courteous and pleasing atmosphere in which all restaurant patrons can enjoy high-quality food at reasonable prices.
Food Items:	The most popular food offering is pizza. Frillio's Pizza also offers a variety of other choices including appetizers, sandwiches, soups, salads, subs, burgers, and desserts.

Using this Book and the Frillio's Pizza Web Site

- Understanding each part of the simulation
- Using the Frillio's Pizza Web site

Understanding Each
Part of the Simulation

Each part of this simulation has been organized into an easy-to-read, step-by-step format. What follows is a brief explanation of the individual sections that make up each part of the simulation. Read it thoroughly to help you become familiar with the format of the book.

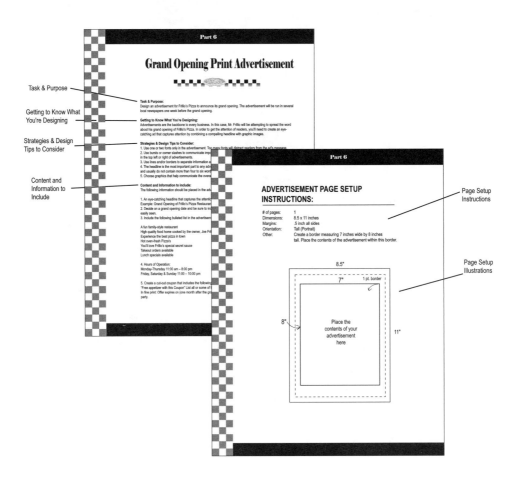

TASK AND PURPOSE:

This section provides you with a detailed description of the document to be created along with the purpose and objectives of how the document will be used by Frillio's Pizza.

OPTIONAL MATERIALS SUGGESTED:

This category is included only if additional supplies can be used to further enhance the final outcome of each document when printed. **Note:** The parts of the simulation that include additional materials are optional and are not required to complete the task.

GETTING TO KNOW WHAT YOU'RE DESIGNING:

This section familiarizes you with the document to be designed in each part of the simulation. A complete description of how each document is used in the business world is provided. *It is strongly recommended that you read this section in each part of the simulation before starting to design the document.*

STRATEGIES AND DESIGN TIPS TO CONSIDER:

This section provides you with design tips, page layout advice, and ideas and suggestions to consider before creating each document. By reading this section, you'll get a clear idea of how to design effective, well-planned documents.

CONTENT AND INFORMATION TO INCLUDE:

This section provides detailed instructions and specifications as to what information should be included in each document. Also included in many parts throughout the simulation are suggested or required graphic images to include on each document.

DESIGN-DEFENSE MEMO (OPTIONAL):

In order to explain the design of each document, you might be asked to type a brief letter of memorandum addressed to Joe Frillio explaining your design, layout scheme, typeface (font) selection, and graphic images.

This is an optional segment for each part of the simulation. Check with your teacher to see if the design-defense memo is required prior to beginning the simulation.

PAGE SETUP INSTRUCTIONS AND ILLUSTRATIONS:

This section provides you with necessary page setup information for each document to be produced. This includes the number of pages, the page dimensions, margin settings, page orientation, other details, and page setup illustrations.

APPROXIMATE COMPLETION TIME:

At the start of each new part of the simulation is the approximate amount of time it should take you to complete the document.

The total approximate time it should take you to complete the entire simulation, including the bonus parts, is 26.5-37 hours. The completion time may vary based on your desktop publishing skill level.

Using the Frillio's Pizza Web Site

Go to FrilliosPizza.com to:
- Download Frillio's Pizza Logos
- Get Free Restaurant-related Clipart
- Download Forms
- Access a Plateful of Great Tools

In addition to this book, a special Frillio's Pizza Web site has been set up to assist you in the production and design of each document you will be asked to create.

To access the Frillio's Pizza Web site, simply point your browser to *www.frilliospizza.com*.

THE FRILLIO'S PIZZA WEB SITE INCLUDES THE FOLLOWING:

■ The Frillio's Pizza Official Logo

Depending on your teacher's instructions, you can either download the official Frillio's Pizza logo, or you can design your own.

The Frillio's Pizza logo is available for download in a variety of file formats (see the Web site for available formats). Before download-ing the logo, check with your teacher to see what file format is compat-ible with your desktop publishing software.

In addition to the logo, you will also find downloads of Joe Frillio and other Frillio's Pizza graphics such as a checkered background and the MasterCard®, Visa®, and American Express® logos, which you will need later on in the simulation.

All of the logos and other Frillio's Pizza graphics can be found under the logos link at the top of the homepage.

■ Free Pizza Restaurant-Related Clipart

Courtesy of Clipart.com™, the Frillio's Pizza Web site includes hundreds of free pizza restaurant-related clipart images available for download and use in your documents.

The clipart is organized in a variety of categories such as pizza, equipment, and beverages. The clipart is available for download in .wmf format, which is compatible with most desktop publishing software.

The free clipart can be accessed by visiting the Frillio's Pizza Web site and clicking on the "clipart" link.

■ Forms

It is recommended that you use the Frillio's Pizza Document Planning Sheet to create a thumbnail sketch of each document before starting its design on the computer. This form, along with any others required in the simulation, can be downloaded from the Frillio's Pizza Web site.

■ Other Good Stuff

There's also a host of other tools that you will find very helpful in producing professional documents that sizzle with creativity and pizza-pizzazz!

Tips and Guidelines for Designing Great Documents

- Desktop Publishing Design Tips and Guidelines
- Document Planning Sheet
- Elements and Shapes That Inspire Great Design
- Words and Phrases That Help Sell Pizza

Desktop Publishing
Design Tips and Guidelines

Whether you're an experienced graphic designer or you're just getting started, the following desktop publishing design tips and guidelines will help you in the preparation of each document in the Frillio's Pizza simulation. Careful preparation, planning, and following these guidelines will get you cooking-up professional, attractive, and eye-catching documents that you'll be glad to showcase.

For starters, let's take a look at what makes a well-designed document effective. The following is a checklist of items that will make a document sparkle and shine with professionalism and creativity:

- The document is attractive and pleasing to look at and read.
- The document is well-organized.
- The document is self-explanatory.
- The text and imagery are carefully linked to each other.
- The design and content are appropriate for the targeted audience.

What follows are some fundamental desktop publishing design tips, guidelines, and advice to follow as you produce each document throughout the simulation. Following these tips and guidelines will help you to produce top-notch professional documents.

■ KNOW YOUR AUDIENCE

Determine the single most important message of your document by asking yourself: If my viewer carries away one idea, what do I want it to be? The answer will be the central theme that determines your entire document design.

■ WHITE SPACE

White space is the area of a document not covered by text or graphics. The general rule of thumb when considering white space is to not have too much or the viewer's eye will wander and to not have too little or you'll confuse and overwhelm your viewer. A guideline to follow is that if your page looks cluttered, eliminate the least important text and/or graphic images from the page.

■ WORKING WITH TYPEFACES (FONTS) AND TYPE STYLES

Take a look at your favorite magazine or book. Chances are they contain no more than three or four typefaces (more commonly referred to as fonts) in total. Too many typefaces or fonts will make your document look cluttered, unprofessional, as well as making it difficult to read.

As a rule, stick to using no more than a total of two to three fonts per document. Select one font that will serve as the primary font (used for areas that contain more than two or three sentences in one area) and one font to serve as your secondary font (used for areas that are headlines, headings, or subheadings).

Here are some general guidelines to follow when working with typefaces (fonts) and type styles:

- Font size should be kept between 18-24 points for headlines, 14-16 points for subheadings, and between 10-12 points for text used in the body areas of a document.
- When considering type styles, with the exception of titles, avoid using all capital letters.
- Avoid excessive use of underlines, italics, and boldface text.
- Select a typeface (font) that is appropriate to the document's subject.
- Be consistent with your typeface (font) choices throughout each document in the simulation. This will help to establish a consistent look adding to the professionalism of the document.

■ KEEP DOCUMENT DESIGN SYMMETRICAL AND PROPORTIONAL

Creating balance and symmetry throughout a document is critical to its final appearance. If, for example, you are creating a document that contains three separate headings, keep the type size of the headings relatively the same. Otherwise, your document will look out of proportion giving it an amateur look and feel.

Follow these guidelines to keep your documents looking balanced and in proportion:

- Use the same typefaces (fonts) throughout each document to give the document a crisp, clean, consistent look.
- If using columns, keep the width and the distance between each column the same.
- Use the same style and size of graphic images.
- Use the same type size for different headings and the same type size for body areas.

■ MARGINS AND SPACING

All edges and margins of a document should be straight and even. Don't overcrowd space, and be attentive to balance content from top-to-bottom and side-margin to side-margin. If possible, organize your text into columns, rather than stretching it across the page. This will make the text easier to read and give the document a more balanced appearance.

■ WORKING WITH GRAPHIC IMAGES

You've heard it a million times, "a picture is worth a thousand words." How true this is when it comes to document design. When selecting graphic images, try choosing those that have the same look and style. For instance, let's say you're designing the Frillio's Pizza menu and you've selected a graphic image of a pizza that has a photographic style. Other graphics that you choose to use in the menu should have the same photographic quality in them. This helps to establish consistency throughout the document and gives it a polished, professional look.

■ ESTABLISH A PROFESSIONAL IDENTITY

When businesses communicate through print, they rely heavily on the look and design of their documents to convey their intended image and identity to consumers.

To help Frillio's Pizza establish a professional image throughout the simulation, you should:

- Use the same typefaces (fonts) throughout the simulation.
- Use the same color scheme (if using a color printer).
- Use the same style of objects and design elements. For example, if you have selected a starburst to highlight important information in one document, consider using the same starburst in other documents.
- Use the same style graphic images.

■ PROOFREAD FOR SPELLING, GRAMMAR AND DESIGN

Nothing spoils a well-designed document more than a typo. When you are nearing the completion of a document, take the time to proofread it for spelling, grammar, and design. Are there any misspelled words? Do the sentences make sense? Did you leave out any required text or design elements? These are the questions to ask before submitting any document.

A good piece of advice is to give your document to one or two people and let them proofread the document. Often they will find an error or omission that you didn't see.

■ REVISE, REVISE, REVISE

Desktop publishing design is much like writing an essay. It almost never comes out right the first time around. Look at your starting point as just that, a starting point. Print your document early on in the design phase and plan on making several revisions, additions, and deletions to attain a professional, well-designed end product.

■ WHEN IN DOUBT, "KIS"

This rule is simple. If you are spending precious time pondering over using one graphic image versus the other or haggling over selecting a particular font, then "KIS."

"KIS" is an acronym commonly used by designers. It stands for "Keep It Simple." When faced with making a decision, always go with the one that is simplest. If, for instance, you are debating whether or not to include a graphic of a slice of pizza or a complex graphic involving a family eating pizza at a dinner table, choose the slice of pizza.

■ USING DESIGN ELEMENTS

On page 20, you'll find a nifty visual entitled *Elements and Shapes That Inspire Great Design.* Refer to this page and experiment with using one or a combination of several of the shapes and elements as you produce each document throughout the simulation.

■ MOST IMPORTANTLY—HAVE A PAPER PLAN

One of the worst habits a desktop publisher or designer can establish is to start designing on a computer without first having a plan on paper. Good design starts on paper first! A sheet of paper, a pencil, and a ruler are the only tools you'll need to get your imagination and creativity steamrolling. Look at it this way—it is much easier, and faster, to experiment with shapes, graphics, text styles, and borders on a piece of paper than on a computer.

Use a planning form similar to the one provided on page 19 to plan each document on paper first. You should use this form for every part of the simulation. You can obtain copies of this form by downloading and printing it from the Frillio's Pizza Web site by visiting *www.frilliospizza.com*.

Unless otherwise noted, the document planning sheet should be completed as the first step in designing each document in the simulation. You can download this form by visiting the Frillio's Pizza Web site at *www.frilliospizza.com*.

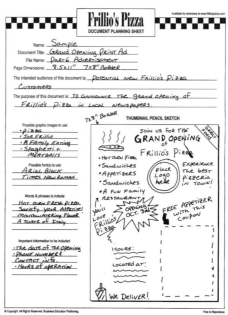

■ **WORKING IN BLACK & WHITE OR COLOR**

Consider the following guidelines if you will be printing your documents using a **color printer***:*

To help Frillio's Pizza establish a professional image, you'll want to use a common color scheme throughout the simulation. The rule for color is to select one or two colors maximum. If you choose to use two colors, use one as a primary color and the second as an accent color. Think of a house. The body is the primary color, and the trim is the accent color.

Try to select colors that match. Think about choosing colors like you do when you pick out your outfit for school or work each day. You try to select a coordinated color scheme. The same principle applies to desktop publishing design.

Consider the following guidelines, if you will be using a **monochrome** *(black ink only) printer:*

Don't underestimate the power of using black ink only, and remember that white is also a color. In fact, when you use black ink printers, you are actually using two colors— black and the color of the paper you are printing on. When working with monochrome printers, try using tints, also referred to as gray scale, to produce contrast and a variation of color.

Frillio's Pizza

DOCUMENT PLANNING SHEET

Name: _____

Document Title: _____

File Name: _____

Page Dimensions: _____

The intended audience of this document is: _____

_____

The purpose of this document is: _____

_____

THUMBNAIL PENCIL SKETCH

Possible graphic images to use:

_____
_____
_____
_____
_____

Possible font(s) to use:

_____
_____
_____

Words and phrases to include:

_____
_____
_____
_____
_____

Important information to be included:

_____
_____
_____
_____
_____

Elements and Shapes That Inspire Great Design

The shapes and elements on this page can be easily made using today's desktop publishing software. Experiment with using them in each document throughout the simulation.

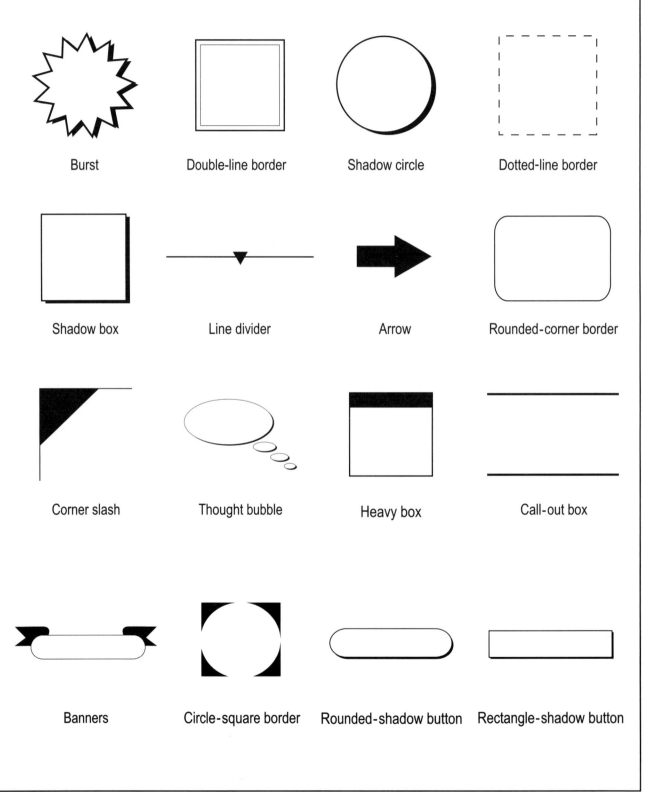

Burst

Double-line border

Shadow circle

Dotted-line border

Shadow box

Line divider

Arrow

Rounded-corner border

Corner slash

Thought bubble

Heavy box

Call-out box

Banners

Circle-square border

Rounded-shadow button

Rectangle-shadow button

Make Your Content Come Alive!

When businesses create documents for customers, be it a basic customer welcome letter, or an elaborate print advertisement, the focus is always on creating an attractive, well-organized, interesting message. The information inside of a document (referred to as *content*) is just as, if not more important, than its design.

As you create each of the documents for Frillio's Pizza, pay careful attention to the words and phrases that you choose to include. Your selection of adjectives, language style, and the meanings of the words should be carefully planned and crafted to bring out the targeted emotion of the document.

The following list of words and phrases will help you to develop great content for each document throughout the simulation. For example, when designing the grand opening print advertisement, consider using words that capture the sense of smell and taste for pizza such as "Frillio's Pizza is Cooked to Perfection!"

Words and Phrases That Make
Food-Related Documents Come Alive!

Note: Words or phrases that have dot leaders (…) and blank spaces (_____) in them are set up for you to experiment with different words that fit the phrase or meaning.

_____ tastes so good, it's addictive	Crisp
A _____ by any other name would never taste the same	Crispy Crust
A burst of flavor	Crust
A commitment to service	Dazzling
A delicious indulgence	Delicious
A feast of…	Delicious flavor
An especially appealing…	Excellent
Attention!	Exceptional
Awesome	Family fun
Baked	Fast
Best prices	First class
By popular demand	For extra taste, try…
Call our toll-free number…	Friendly
Celebrate the…	Friendly service
Cheerful	Friendly staff
Cheesy-to-the-Max	Generous portion of…
Chock full of…	Generously sized
Colossal	Gigantic
Cooked-to-Perfection	Good News!
Courteous	Grand Opening!
	Great
	Great family fun

(continued...)

Words and Phrases That Make Food-Related Documents Come Alive!

Great-tasting
Hearty helping
Highest quality
Hits the spot
Homemade taste
Hot out of the oven…
Hot-Oven-Fresh
Huge
Included at no extra cost
Irresistible
It will tempt your palate
It's all here!
It's hot, hot, hot!
King-size
Loaded with...
Love at first bite
Made for you to enjoy
Mouthwatering
New!
No additives
No artificial flavors
Nobody beats…
Nothing pleases all your senses
  like a good pizza!
Old family recipe
One-of-a-kind
Original recipe
Our customers always come first
Our reputation for…
Our specialty is your satisfaction
Outstanding
Oven-fresh
Packed with…
Perfected
Pizza-packed
Primo
Prize-winning
Quick
Reputable
Satisfies your need for…

Satisfy your appetite
Satisfying
Savory
Scrumptious
Seasoned with…
Sensational
Smell the difference
Special
Special grand opening offer!
Spectacular
Stuffed with…
Sumptuous
Superb
Superior flavor
Supreme
Surpassingly…
Taste it all
Taste it and see
Tastes as good as it looks
Tastes great!
Tasty
Terrific
The best deal in town
The biggest
The finest…
The foremost…
The greatest…
The one and only…
The taste that _____
The ultimate…
Top-notch
Treat yourself to a…
Unlike any other…
We take great pride in…
We think you'll agree…
We're dedicated to…
We're looking forward to seeing you.
Where the flavor is
Zesty

It's Time to Warm-up
Your Pizza-Design Skills

In order to create and design the documents for the owner of a pizza establishment, you'll need to learn how to think like one. To help get your creative juices flowing and your pizza-design skills sizzling, try the following two warm-up exercises before proceeding to part 1 of the simulation.

Both exercises will help familiarize you with the pizzeria restaurant industry. The first gets you thinking about pizza; the second gets you thinking about restaurant-related food images.

WARM-UP EXERCISE #1: PIZZA BRAINSTORMING

OBJECTIVE:
To get your mind and your imagination ready for pizza-designing by creating a list of words, phrases, and objects that relate to a pizza restaurant.

INSTRUCTIONS:

1.   Using desktop publishing or word processing software, open a new document. Using the text tool, create a list of at least 25 words, phrases, and/or objects that relate to a pizza restaurant.

When creating the list, think about images, words, and objects that you have seen or heard in a restaurant. To galvanize your thoughts, try to envsion the images you have seen when you have dined at a restaurant. You should start to see images of a kitchen, appliances such as a stove, dining tables, window signs, newspaper advertisements, a waiter's tray, and so on.

2.   Separate the list into two columns. Save the document as "Pizza list." Print the document, and keep this list handy as you create each document throughout the simulation. Refer to the list when you are at a loss for words, when you need an idea for a graphic image, or use it to get inspiration for design and creativity.

Remember that this is a brainstorming exercise. Don't be too concerned if a word doesn't form an exact match to a pizza restaurant, just list all the words that come to your mind.

To help you get started, here are five possibilities:

1. Sauce
2. Toppings
3. Pizza box
4. Pizza cutter
5. Apron

WARM-UP EXERCISE #2:
PIZZA RESTAURANT FONTS, GRAPHICS, AND HEADLINES

OBJECTIVE:
To help you develop eye-catching headlines and graphic images that you can use in various documents throughout the Frillio's Pizza simulation.

INSTRUCTIONS:

1. Using your desktop publishing software, open a new document. Using the text tool, key the list shown below into separate text boxes. Assume that each item in the list represents a different headline being used in a document.
    Arrange the list neatly into columns on your page. Experiment with changing the typeface (font), size, and style of each headline.

Grand Opening
Hot Oven Fresh Pizza
Mouthwatering Taste
Friendly Service
Cooked to Perfection!
Win a FREE T-shirt!
We Deliver Every Day and Evening of the Week
Delicious Sandwiches
Treat Yourself to a Dessert
Mozzarella Sticks that Melt in Your Mouth
Frillio's Special Sauce
Join the Pizza Club
Thank You for Dining at Frillio's Pizza
Order from Our Takeout Menu
Fun for the Kiddies!
Enjoy a FREE beverage with the purchase of one large pizza

---

2. Underneath each headline, place an appropriate graphic that helps to illustrate each headline.

3. Save the document as "Headline and Graphics." Print the document, and use it to help you in the production of each document throughout the simulation.

Part 1:
Design or Download the
Frillio's Pizza Logo

Approximate Completion Time: .5 - 2 hours

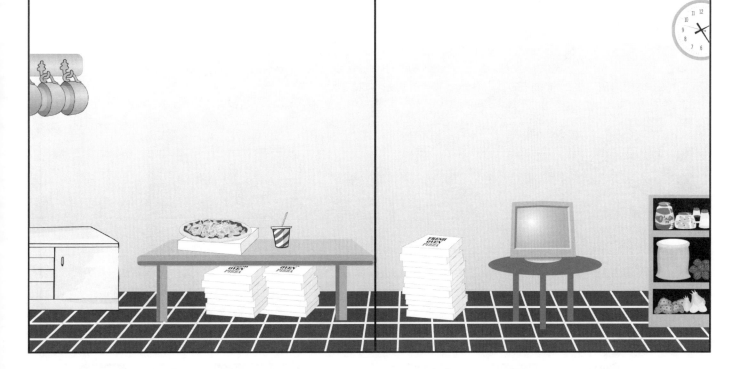

Download or Create
the Frillio's Pizza Logo

TASK AND PURPOSE:

To help Frillio's Pizza establish a professional business image and to become easily recognizable in the minds of consumers, create and design a logo for Frillio's Pizza. Or, download the official Frillio's Pizza logo from the Frillio's Pizza Web site at *www.frilliospizza.com.*

GETTING TO KNOW WHAT YOU'RE DESIGNING:

A logo is a name, symbol, emblem, or trademark designed for easy and definite recognition. In short, a logo is one of the most important elements in defining an image for a company. A logo can contain text, graphics, or a combination of both.

STRATEGIES AND DESIGN TIPS TO CONSIDER BEFORE CREATING YOUR LOGO:
Note: You can skip this section if you will be downloading the Frillio's Pizza logo.

1. Be sure that your logo is not too complex. The best logos are those that are easy to read and recognize.
2. Use only one typeface (font) in the logo.
3. A logo should look good at any size. Keep in mind that your logo will be included in just about every document throughout this simulation.
4. Consider using the Frillio's Pizza slogan, "The best pizzeria in town," in your logo design.
5. Develop three to five different versions of your logo. Seek the opinions of your instructor and classmates to help you select the final version of the logo to use throughout the remainder of the simulation.

INSTRUCTIONS:

Depending on your teacher's instructions, you have two options to consider in this section.

OPTION 1: DOWNLOAD THE LOGO

You can visit the Frillio's Pizza Web site at *www.frilliospizza.com* to download the official Frillio's Pizza logo. It can be downloaded in a variety of different file formats, sizes, and colors. Check with your teacher to see what file formats will work best with your desktop publishing software. Other graphic images such as the Frillio's Pizza text and Joe Frillio are also available on the Web site.

Visit *www.frilliospizza.com* to download the Frillio's Pizza logo and other logo-related images to use throughout the rest of the simulation

OPTION 2: CREATE YOUR OWN FRILLIO'S PIZZA LOGO

Create a sketch of your logo design on paper first. Be sure that the logo includes the text "Frillio's Pizza" prominently displayed on it.

Since the logo will be used as a graphic image in every document throughout the simulation, it might be best to create your logo using an illustration or drawing software program.

As previously noted, it is recommended that you develop three to five different versions of your logo. Seek the opinions of your instructor and classmates to help you select the final version of the logo to use throughout the remainder of the simulation.

Possible graphic images to consider using in your logo are:
A slice of pizza
A whole pizza
A checkered tablecloth pattern

Save the document as: Part 1 Logo

Optional Design-Defense Memo:
Type a letter of memorandum addressed to Joe Frillio explaining your design, placement, font selections, layout scheme, and choice of graphic image(s). Attach this memo to your final document.

Part 2:
Design the Frillio's
Pizza Stationery

- **2A: Letterhead**
- **2B: Envelope**
- **2C: Business Card**

Approximate Completion Time: 1.5 hours

In parts 2A, 2B, and 2C, you will design and create the stationery for Frillio's Pizza which will consist of letterhead, envelopes, and business cards. These items will be used by Frillio's Pizza when communicating with customers and vendors.

Design the Frillio's Pizza Letterhead

TASK AND PURPOSE:

To design and create letterhead stationery that Frillio's Pizza will use to communicate with vendors and customers.

GETTING TO KNOW WHAT YOU'RE DESIGNING:

A letterhead is a sheet of stationery with the name, address, logo and sometimes other relevant information of an organization printed at the top, bottom, left or right side. The standard size of letterhead is 8.5 X 11 inches. Letterhead is used to send business letters and other forms of correspondence.

STRATEGIES AND DESIGN TIPS TO CONSIDER BEFORE CREATING YOUR LETTERHEAD:

1. Keep the design of the letterhead professional, clean, and simple. The sole purpose of letterhead documents is to communicate information. Therefore, the design should be kept simple and professional looking.
2. Most letterhead designs fall within the first 2.5 inches from the top of the page, but you can try experimenting with placing it elsewhere.
3. Stick to using one typeface (font) in the letterhead, except the typeface used in the logo (if you have designed your own).
4. Try to create a balanced, symmetrical look when designing the letterhead. Type should be kept to a maximum of 10 or 12 point sizes.
5. Since the logo is the most important element on a letterhead, it should be the largest item.
6. Try using a thin line to create separation from the letterhead design and the rest of the page.
7. Use the document planning sheet to sketch a thumbnail design of your letterhead on paper first.

CONTENT AND INFORMATION TO INCLUDE ON YOUR LETTERHEAD:

1. The Frillio's Pizza logo.

2. Include the following contact information:

Address:	111 Pepperoni Drive • Saucy, CA 92888
Phone Number:	1-888-FRILLIO
Fax Number:	1-888-654-7814
E-mail address:	Owner@FrilliosPizza.com
Web site address:	http://www.frilliospizza.com

3. Place your name, the document title, and "Part 2A" on the letterhead.

Save the document as: Part 2A Letterhead

Optional Design-Defense Memo:
Type a letter of memorandum addressed to Joe Frillio explaining your design, placement, font selections, layout scheme, and choice of graphic image(s). Attach this memo to your final document.

LETTERHEAD PAGE SETUP INSTRUCTIONS:

# of pages: 1
Dimensions: 8.5 x 11 inches
Margins: .5 inch on all sides
Orientation: Tall (Portrait)

8.5"

Place the contents of your
letterhead here

11"

Design the Frillio's Pizza Envelope

TASK AND PURPOSE:

To design and create a #10 business-size envelope for Frillio's Pizza that coordinates with the letterhead you created in Part 2A.

OPTIONAL MATERIALS SUGGESTED:

A #10 business-size envelope.

GETTING TO KNOW WHAT YOU'RE DESIGNING:

An envelope is used to send a letter and/or other documents. An envelope contains the company name and address in the top left-hand corner (return address area) and the recipient's address in the center. The standard size of a business envelope (also known as a #10 envelope) is 4.125 inches tall x 9.5 inches wide.

STRATEGIES AND DESIGN TIPS TO CONSIDER BEFORE CREATING YOUR ENVELOPE:

1. To establish a consistent, professional image for Frillio's Pizza, the envelope should be a mirror-image of the letterhead design, with the exception of where the information is placed.
2. Place the contents of the return address 1/4 inch in from the top-left edge of the envelope.
3. Obtain some samples of real business envelopes and analyze them to help you design your own.
4. Use the document planning sheet to sketch a thumbnail design of your envelope on paper first.

CONTENT AND INFORMATION TO INCLUDE ON YOUR ENVELOPE:

1. Place the following return address 1/4 inch in from the top-left edge of the envelope:

   The Frillo's Pizza Logo
   111 Pepperoni Drive
   Saucy, CA 92888

2. To add realism to the design of the envelope, place a graphic of a postage stamp in the top right-hand corner.

3. Place your name and school address in the recipient address area on the envelope.

4. Optional: Print the document on a #10 business envelope. See the page setup instructions below and your printer manual for assistance on printing on a real envelope.

Save the document as: Part 2B Envelope

Optional Design-Defense Memo:
Type a letter of memorandum addressed to Joe Frillio explaining your design, placement, font selections, layout scheme, and choice of graphic image(s). Attach this memo to your final document.

ENVELOPE PAGE SETUP INSTRUCTIONS:

Follow these instructions if you will NOT be printing on a real envelope.
Otherwise, see the instructions shown below to print on a real envelope.

# of pages:	1
Dimensions:	11 x 8.5 inches
Margins:	.5 inch on all sides
Orientation:	Wide (Landscape)
Other:	Place a one-point thick rectangular border measuring 9.5 inches wide by 4.125 inches tall. The border will represent the envelope on your page. Use scissors to trim around the border of the envelope.

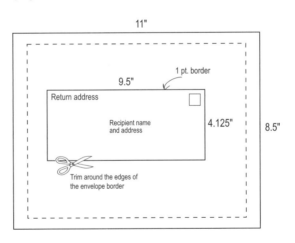

If printing on a real envelope, set up your page as follows:

# of pages:	1
Dimensions:	9.5 inches wide x 4.125 inches tall
Margins:	.25 inches on all sides
Orientation:	Wide (Landscape)
Other:	Consult your printer's manual or see your instructor on how to place a #10 business envelope in your printer.

Design Joe Frillio's Business Card

TASK AND PURPOSE:

To complete the Frillio's Pizza stationery, design and create a business card for Joe Frillio, the owner of Frillio's Pizza.

OPTIONAL MATERIALS SUGGESTED:

Cardstock paper.

GETTING TO KNOW WHAT YOU'RE DESIGNING:

A business card is a small card printed or engraved usually containing a person's name, business affiliation, job title, address, telephone number, e-mail address, and Web site address. The purpose of a business card is to announce one's identity, presence, and the intention to conduct business. The business card is perhaps the most widely used mini-document in the business world. A business card is the handshake you leave behind after meeting someone in the professional world.

STRATEGIES AND DESIGN TIPS TO CONSIDER BEFORE CREATING YOUR BUSINESS CARD:

1. Since a business card does not offer much room, it's important to plan its design carefully.
2. The overall look and feel of the business card should match the type of job you are selecting. A business card designed for a lawyer would have a prestigious, professional look; whereas a comedian's business card would have a fun, humorous look.
3. Consider using lines or borders to help create a balanced look and feel on your business card.
4. Stick to using one typeface (font) to create a crisp, clean, easy-to-read business card.
5. Obtain some samples of real business cards and analyze them to help you design your own.
6. Use the document planning sheet to sketch a thumbnail design of your business card on paper first.

CONTENT AND INFORMATION TO INCLUDE ON YOUR BUSINESS CARD:

1. The Frillio's Pizza logo.

2. The following contact information:

Name and Job Title:	Mr. Joe Frillio, Owner and Pizza-Maker Extraordinaire
Address:	111 Pepperoni Drive, Saucy, CA 92888
Phone Number:	1-888-FRILLIO
Fax Number:	1-888-654-7814
Web site:	http://www.frilliospizza.com
E-mail address:	Owner@FrilliosPizza.com

3. Write your name, the document title, and "Part 2C" on the reverse side of the business card.

Save the document as: Part 2C Business Card

Optional Design-Defense Memo:
Type a letter of memorandum addressed to Joe Frillio explaining your design, placement, font selections, layout scheme, and choice of graphic image(s). Attach this memo to your final document.

BUSINESS CARD PAGE SETUP INSTRUCTIONS:

# of pages: 1
Dimensions: 8.5 x 11 inches
Margins: 1 inch on all sides
Orientation: Tall (Portrait)
Other: Using the rectangle tool in your desktop publishing software, draw a rectangle that measures 3.5 inches wide by 2 inches high. Place the rectangle in the center of the page. Place the contents of the business card within this border. Use scissors to cut around the border of the business card when complete.

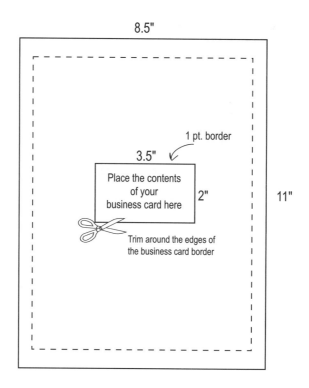

8.5"

1 pt. border

3.5"

Place the contents
of your
business card here

2"

11"

Trim around the edges of
the business card border

Part 3:
Design the Frillio's
Pizza Place Mat

Approximate Completion Time: 2-4 hours

Design the Frillio's Pizza Place Mat

TASK AND PURPOSE:

To design and create a paper place mat that will be used by Frillio's Pizza's restaurant patrons—especially children. In keeping with the spirit and atmosphere of a family-style pizzeria, Mr. Frillio would like you to design place mats that will help keep young children entertained while they wait for their food.

OPTIONAL MATERIALS SUGGESTED:

Colored paper.

GETTING TO KNOW WHAT YOU'RE DESIGNING:

In addition to providing a protective table mat for dishes and flatware, place mats also offer restaurants additional opportunities: a chance to advertise food specials, communicate messages, and entertain children while they wait for their food.

STRATEGIES AND DESIGN TIPS TO CONSIDER BEFORE CREATING YOUR PLACE MAT:

1. Consider using one or more of the following list of kid's activities on your place mat:
   - A pizza word scramble
   - A word search using pizza restaurant-related terms such as soda, sauce, toppings, etc.
   - Instructions asking the children to draw a picture of an object such as a pizza, an animal, or any other kid-friendly object
   - A maze
   - A picture to color
   - A fill in the blanks activity
   - A word match using pizza and restaurant-related words
   - A list of fun facts about pizza
2. Keep the design of the place mat simple. Remember, your audience for the place mat is children.
3. Kids like variety. Experiment with the use of "fun" typefaces (fonts) and styles.
4. Obtain some samples of real place mats and analyze them to help you design your own.
5. Use the document planning sheet to sketch a thumbnail design of your place mat on paper first.

CONTENT AND INFORMATION TO INCLUDE ON YOUR PLACE MAT:

1. Create a fun and easy-to-read title for the place mat. Keep the headline simple; remember, the audience of the place mat is young children.

2. Use your imagination to create several appropriate activities that children can play such as a word search, a maze, or a picture to color.

3. Add appropriate graphic images that help make the place mat fun and appealing to children.

4. Add some kid-humor to the place mat by adding the following one-line jokes:

    > Q: How do you fix a broken pizza?
    > A: With tomato paste.
    >
    > Q: What do you call a person who can drink soda and sing at the same time?
    > A: A pop singer!
    >
    > Q: What do you have when you eat four pieces of cake and six pieces of pizza, all in one meal?
    > A: A tummy ache!
    >
    > Q: What does an aardvark like on its pizza?
    > A: Ant-chovies.
    >
    > Once a scrambled egg walked into Frillio's Pizza. He asked the waiter if he could have something to drink. The waiter said "Sorry, we don't serve breakfast."

5. Include instructions for the children that explain how to complete each activity you have included on your place mat. For example, if you include a maze, clearly mark the start and the end points of the maze.

6. Include the Frillio's Pizza logo on the place mat.

7. Include the following contact information in a visible area on the place mat:

Address:	111 Pepperoni Drive, Saucy, CA 92888
Phone:	1-888-FRILLIO
Web site:	http://www.frilliospizza.com

8. Place the text "We Deliver Every Day and Night of the Week" near the bottom center of the place mat.

9. Include the Frillio's Pizza hours of operation which are:

Mon - Thurs 11 am - 9 pm
Fri, Sat, & Sun 11 am - 10 pm

10. Place your name, the document title, and "Part 3" on the place mat.

Save the document as: Part 3 Place Mat

> **Optional Design-Defense Memo:**
> Type a letter of memorandum addressed to Joe Frillio explaining your design, placement, font selections, layout scheme, and choice of graphic image(s). Attach this memo to your final document.

PLACE MAT PAGE SETUP INSTRUCTIONS:

# of pages:	1
Dimensions:	11 x 8.5 inches
Margins:	.25 inches on all sides
Orientation:	Landscape (Wide)
Other:	Place the contents of your place mat within a 10.5 inch wide x 8 inch tall border.

11"
1 pt. border
10.5"

Place the contents of your
place mat here

8"   8.5"

Part 4:
Design a
Coupon Flyer

Approximate Completion Time: 2-3 hours

Design a Coupon Flyer

TASK AND PURPOSE:

To encourage restaurant patrons to return to Frillio's Pizza, Mr. Frillio would like you to design and create a flyer containing coupons that will be placed in a variety of areas throughout his restaurant including each dinner table, the checkout counter, and display boxes.

OPTIONAL MATERIALS SUGGESTED:

Colored paper.

GETTING TO KNOW WHAT YOU'RE DESIGNING:

A flyer can take on a variety of formats, sizes, and designs. The purpose of a flyer is to communicate a message in a limited amount of space. Flyers can be used to announce events, advertise a product or service, or promote a cause. The primary objective of a flyer is to capture the reader's attention.

STRATEGIES AND DESIGN TIPS TO CONSIDER BEFORE CREATING YOUR FLYER:

1. Since most readers tend to look at flyers as non-reading documents, keep text to a minimum. Do, however, provide enough information to keep the reader's attention.
2. Keep the number of typefaces (fonts) to a maximum of three.
3. When choosing graphics, it will be more effective to include one or two larger graphics than to clutter the page with numerous small graphics.
4. When creating the coupons, use a dotted-line border with a small graphic of scissors placed on one of the border sides to encourage customers to cut out and use the coupons.
5. Create a balanced and symmetrical look throughout the flyer by using the same size border for each of the four coupons you will be creating.
6. Obtain some samples of coupon flyers from your local newspaper and analyze them to help you design your own.
7. Use the document planning sheet to sketch a thumbnail design of your coupon flyer on paper first.

CONTENT AND INFORMATION TO INCLUDE ON YOUR COUPON FLYER:

1. A simple-to-read headline.

    Examples: "Thank You for Dining at Frillio's"
    "Please Join Us Again"
    "Great Offers for Your Next Meal at Frillio's Pizza"

2. Include four cut-out style coupons, each containing the headline and subtext on the indicated coupon number shown below. Add one small graphic image to enhance the look and appeal of each coupon.

    Coupon #1: *Headline*: FREE BEVERAGE
    Subtext: Enjoy a FREE beverage with the purchase of one
    large pizza when you present this coupon.
    Coupon #2: *Headline*: FREE MEDIUM PIZZA
    Subtext: One FREE medium pizza when you order two large
    pizzas when you present this coupon.
    Coupon #3: *Headline*: SAVE $5
    Subtext: Take $5 off of the total of your next meal or
    takeout order when you present this coupon.
    Good on orders of $20 or more.
    Coupon #4: *Headline*: FREE APPETIZER
    Subtext: Get one FREE appetizer with the purchase of any
    Frillio's sandwich when you present this coupon.

3. Using a small type size, add the text "Limit: one coupon per party" to each of the four coupons shown above.

4. Add an expiration date to each of the four coupons.

5. Include the Frillio's Pizza logo and the following contact information on the flyer:

    Address: 111 Pepperoni Drive, Saucy, CA 92888
    Phone Number: 1-888-FRILLIO
    Web site: http://www.frilliospizza.com
    E-mail: Owner@FrilliosPizza.com

6. Include the Frillio's Pizza hours of operation which are:

    Mon - Thurs 11 am - 9 pm
    Fri, Sat, & Sun 11 am - 10 pm

7. Add the text "We Deliver Every Day and Night of the Week" to the flyer.

8. Add additional text or graphic images that will help make the coupon flyer achieve the objective of getting customers to return to Frillio's Pizza.

9. Place your name, the document title, and "Part 4" on the flyer.

Save the document as: Part 4 Coupon Flyer

Optional Design-Defense Memo:
Type a letter of memorandum addressed to Joe Frillio explaining your design, placement, font selections, layout scheme, and choice of graphic image(s). Attach this memo to your final document.

COUPON FLYER PAGE SETUP INSTRUCTIONS:

# of pages: 1
Dimensions: 8.5 x 11 inches
Margins: 1 inch on all sides
Orientation: Portrait (Tall)

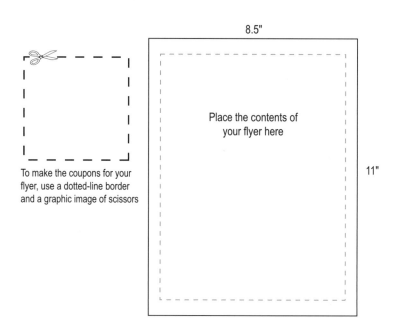

To make the coupons for your flyer, use a dotted-line border and a graphic image of scissors

8.5"

Place the contents of your flyer here

11"

Part 5:
Design the
Frillio's Pizza Menu

Approximate Completion Time: 3-5 hours

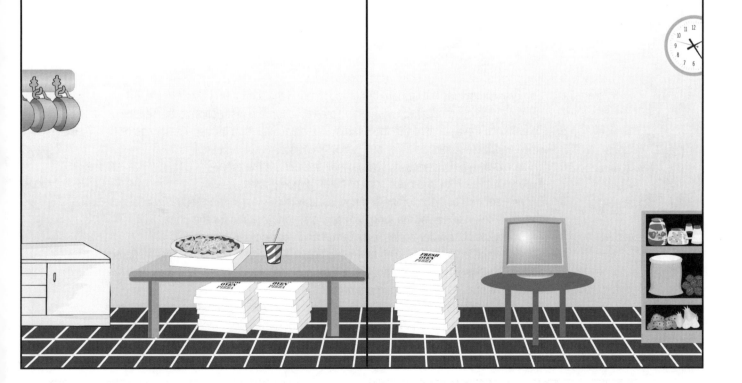

Design the Frillio's Pizza Menu

TASK AND PURPOSE:

To create and design a booklet-style menu for Frillio's Pizza. Of all the documents Mr. Frillio needs created, the menu will be the most visible and highly profiled. The menu will be the one document that every restaurant patron will see.

OPTIONAL MATERIALS SUGGESTED:

Colored paper.

GETTING TO KNOW WHAT YOU'RE DESIGNING:

A menu is a list of food items offered by a restaurant. Menus take on a variety of shapes, sizes, and colors. Most menus are laminated to help protect them from food and drink spills. The typical menu consists of appetizers, main entrees, desserts, and beverages. A menu is the signature of a restaurant. It is the one document that every customer will see and read. Most restaurants hire professional graphic designers to handle the creation of their menus. Careful planning, thought, and page layout is the key to successful menu design.

STRATEGIES AND DESIGN TIPS TO CONSIDER BEFORE CREATING YOUR MENU:

1. Try using at least two different typefaces (fonts). One font should be for the menu items and their prices, another for a subtext that describes the menu items.
2. Highlight the most important items using a boldface typestyle.
3. Keep the menu clean, uncluttered, and legible.
4. Use graphic images throughout the menu to bring the food items listed to life. Be careful not to overdo it. Too many graphics will become a distraction to the reader.
5. To enhance the appeal of the food items, use adjectives that trigger the senses of smell and taste. Example: "Try our perfectly-seasoned spinach pies."
6. Try to create a balanced, symmetrical look throughout the menu.
7. Type should be kept to a maximum of 10 or 12 point sizes.
8. Experiment with using columns when working with the text in the menu. Try a layout that uses one column for the food item and a second column for the price.
9. Try using lines or border boxes to separate each category in the menu.
10. Consider where you are placing the menu items. Appetizers almost always go first on a menu because they tend to bring in a high profit for a restaurant, and they are usually the first food item customers order.
11. Experiment with different tab settings. Tabs will allow you to connect each menu item with its price while providing enough space between them for easy reading. Tabs set

with dot leaders (a row of dots or periods) is an eye-friendly way to connect each food item to its price.

12. Obtain some samples of actual restaurant menus. Analyze the design and style of each, and use them as a guide to create your menu.

13. Hold a blank sheet of paper the long way (landscape) and fold it in half creating a booklet style format. Sketch a thumbnail design of your menu on this paper.

CONTENT AND INFORMATION TO INCLUDE ON YOUR MENU:

Note: The menu will be designed using a booklet-style format printed on two sides. When folded in half the long way (landscape), the menu will be divided into four equal size panels. The information to include on each panel is given below.

Outside Front Panel:
1. Place the word "Menu" using a large text size in the top-center of the outside front panel.

2. Include the Frillio's Pizza logo on the outside front panel.

3. Add the Frillio's Pizza slogan "The best pizzeria in town" to the outside front panel.

4. Add the text "All of our menu items are also available for takeout."

5. Place the following contact information on the bottom center of the outside front panel:

Address:	111 Pepperoni Drive, Saucy, CA 92888
Phone Number:	1-888-FRILLIO
Web site:	http://www.frilliospizza.com

6. Add additional text, design elements, and/or graphic images that will help make the outside front panel of the menu look attractive and professional.

Inside Left and Right Panels:
1. Add the Frillio's Pizza menu items and prices. See pages 52 and 53 for a complete listing of the menu items and prices.

2. If space is an issue, you may place a portion of the menu items and prices on the outside back panel of the menu.

3. Add graphic images of various food items listed to enhance the visual appeal of the menu.

Note: You may not make any changes to the menu items and their prices. You may, however, add catchy adjectives, phrases, and/or descriptions that make the menu items more appealing and appetizing. For example, under the menu item "*Homemade Mozzarella Sticks*" you might add a description that reads "*Breaded, fried, and oozing with cheese.*"

---

4. Add a boxed border to surround the menu items and prices to give the menu a neat appearance.

Outside Back Panel:

1. If more space is needed, you may use the outside back panel to list any menu items and prices not listed on the inside left and right panels.
   Caution: Be sure to keep different categories of menu items together on the same side panel. For example, do not separate the desserts onto two separate sided panels.

2. Place the Frillio's Pizza logo near the bottom of the outside back panel and include a message that reads *"Thank you for dining at Frillio's Pizza. Please come again."*

3. Add the Frillio's Pizza mission statement which is:

   "To provide a courteous and pleasing atmosphere in which all restaurant patrons can enjoy high-quality food at reasonable prices."

4. Include the Frillio's Pizza hours of operation which are:

   Mon - Thurs 11 am - 9 pm
   Fri, Sat, & Sun 11 am - 10 pm

5. Add the text "We accept MasterCard®, Visa®, and American Express® cards." Include a graphic image of each of the MasterCard®, Visa®, and American Express® logos. You can download these logos from the Frillio's Pizza Web site at *www.frilliospizza.com.*

6. Place your name, the document title, and "Part 5" on the menu.

Save the document as: Part 5 Booklet Menu

Optional Design-Defense Memo:
Type a letter of memorandum addressed to Joe Frillio explaining your design, placement, font selections, layout scheme, and choice of graphic image(s). Attach this memo to your final document.

MENU PAGE SETUP INSTRUCTIONS:

# of pages: 2
Dimensions: 11 x 8.5 inches
Margins: .25 inches all sides
Orientation: Wide (Landscape)
Finished size: 5.5 x 8.5 inches
Other: The menu will be created using a booklet-style format printed on both sides of the paper. On both sides of the menu, place vertical page guides at 5.25", 5.5", and 5.75". This will create a .5" gutter space where the menu will be folded. Do not place any contents inside the .5" gutter space on either side of the menu (see the illustration provided below for more help).

Printing Note: Print the menu back-to-back (double-sided) on your printer or print both sheets separately and staple or tape them together.

Page 1 - Outside of Menu

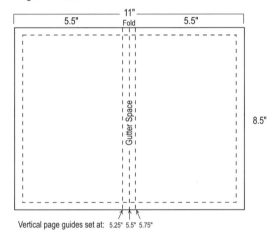

Vertical page guides set at: 5.25" 5.5" 5.75"

Page 2 - Inside of Menu

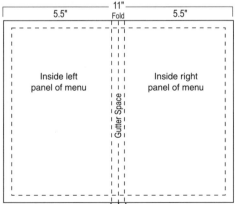

Vertical page guides set at: 5.25" 5.5" 5.75"

When folded, the finished menu should look like this in booklet format.

Frillio's Pizza Menu Items and Prices

MENU ITEM	PRICE

Appetizers & Side Orders

Soup of the Day .... Cup $1.75   Bowl $2.50
Homemade Mozzarella Sticks $4.95
Side Salad $1.95
  Dressing choices: House Italian, Ranch, Parmesan Peppercorn, Fat-free Honey Mustard, Blue Cheese, Balsamic Vinaigrette
Soup and Salad Combo $5.25
Garlic Bread $2.50
Chicken Tenders .... Sm.(4) $4.50   Lg.(8) $7.95
French Fries .... Sm. $1.50 Lg. $1.95

Pizza

The Famous Frillio's Pizza
  Cheese Only .... Sm. $5.99 Med. $7.99 Lg. $10.99
  Additional toppings (add .50 per topping): pepperoni, sausage, mushrooms, peppers,
  olives, meatballs, extra cheese, anchovies, onions, sliced tomato
  Add Frillio's special secret sauce to any pizza for $1.50 extra.

Submarine Sandwiches

Steak & Cheese .... Sm. $3.75 Med. $4.50 Lg. $5.99
Meatball & Cheese .... Sm. $2.90 Med. $3.45 Lg. $4.60
Italian Cold Cut .... Sm. $2.75 Med. $3.10 Lg. $4.25
Ham & Provolone Cheese .... Sm. $2.75 Med. $3.10 Lg. $4.25
Turkey Breast & Cheese .... Sm. $2.75 Med. $3.10 Lg. $4.25
Frillio's Special Sandwich (*secret recipe*) .... Sm. $3.00 Med. $3.40 Lg. $4.60
  All submarine sandwich orders come with choice of fries, cup of soup, or side salad.
  All sandwiches are served on a 7-inch bulky Italian roll. Add lettuce and tomato at no extra charge.

Dishes

Spaghetti & Meatballs $7.95
Chicken Parmigiana $8.95
  Comes with your choice of spaghetti or pasta
Pasta Primavera $7.95
Homemade Stuffed Shells $7.95

Burgers & Sandwiches

The Frillio Burger $7.95
Garden Burger $5.95
Chicken Sandwich $7.95
Gourmet BLT $5.95
  All burger, chicken, and BLT sandwich orders come with choice of fries, cup of soup, or side salad.
  Add a topping: provolone, white American cheese, blue cheese, cheddar, jalapenos or BBQ sauce for .50 extra.
  All sandwiches are served on a fresh bulky Italian roll.

Frillio's Pizza Menu Items and Prices

MENU ITEM	PRICE

Pies

Spinach or Broccoli Pies

    Plain $1.75

    w/ cheese & pepperoni $2.50

Beverages

Coke®, Sprite®, Pepsi®, Root Beer, Diet Coke®, Lemonade, Chocolate Milk .... Sm. $1.50   Lg. $1.75

For The Kiddies

Chicken Fingers & Fries $3.95

Hot Dog & Fries $3.95

Grilled Cheese & Fries $3.95

Desserts

Ooey Gooey Brownie $3.50

Ice Cream

    1 Scoop $1.00

    2 Scoops $1.75

    Choice of homemade vanilla, chocolate, or strawberry topped with hot fudge and whipped cream.

Part 6:
Create the Grand
Opening Advertisement

Approximate Completion Time: 2-3 hours

Create the Grand Opening Advertisement

TASK AND PURPOSE:

To create and design a print advertisement for Frillio's Pizza to announce its grand opening to the public. The advertisement will be run in several local newspapers one week before the grand opening.

GETTING TO KNOW WHAT YOU'RE DESIGNING:

Advertisements are the backbone of every business. In this case, Mr. Frillio will be attempting to spread the word about his grand opening of Frillio's Pizza. In order to get the attention of readers, you'll need to create an eye-catching advertisement that captures attention by combining a compelling headline with graphic images.

STRATEGIES AND DESIGN TIPS TO CONSIDER BEFORE CREATING YOUR ADVERTISEMENT:

1. To create a professional looking advertisement, use only one or two typefaces (fonts) in the advertisement.
2. Use starbursts or corner slashes to communicate important information. Starbursts and corner slashes are usually placed in the top left or right side of advertisements.
3. Use lines and/or borders to separate important information and to make the advertisement easier to read.
4. The headline is the most important part of any advertisement. Headlines are usually the largest element in an ad and usually do not contain more than four to six words.
5. Choose graphics that help communicate the overall message being conveyed. Do not overcrowd the advertisement or it will lose its appeal.
6. Use the document planning sheet to sketch a thumbnail design of your advertisement on paper first.

CONTENT AND INFORMATION TO INCLUDE IN YOUR ADVERTISEMENT:

1. Create an eye-catching headline that captures the attention of prospective readers. Example: *Grand Opening of Frillio's Pizza!*

2. Decide on a grand opening date and include it in the top area of the advertisement where it can be easily seen.

3. Enclose the bullet list shown below with a rectangular or square border and include the headline "You'll Love Frillio's Pizza..." just above the list:

   • A fun family-style restaurant
   • High-quality food, home cooked by the owner, Joe Frillio
   • Experience the best, hot oven-fresh pizza in town
   • Come in and try Frillio's special secret sauce
   • Takeout orders available

4. Include the Frillio's Pizza hours of operation which are:

   Mon - Thurs 11 am - 9 pm
   Fri, Sat, & Sun 11 am - 10 pm

5. Create a cut-out style coupon that includes the following on it:

   • A headline that reads "Free Appetizer"
   • List all or some of the appetizers available on the coupon
     (see the Frillio's menu from part 5)
   • In fine print, include text that reads "Offer expires on _____
     (one month after the grand opening date you decided on).
     Limit: one appetizer per party."

6. Include the Frillo's Pizza logo on the advertisement.

7. Include the following contact information:

   Address: 111 Pepperoni Drive, Saucy, CA 92888
   Phone Number: 1-888-FRILLIO
   Web site: http://www.frilliospizza.com

8. Choose one or two graphic images that help illustrate and enhance the look of the content in the advertisement.

9. Add any additional information you feel will be helpful in getting customers to react to the advertisement.

10. Place your name, the document title, and "Part 6" on the advertisement.

Save the document as: Part 6 Advertisement

Optional Design-Defense Memo:
Type a letter of memorandum addressed to Joe Frillio explaining your design, placement, font selections, layout scheme, and choice of graphic image(s). Attach this memo to your final document.

ADVERTISEMENT PAGE SETUP INSTRUCTIONS:

# of pages:	1
Dimensions:	8.5 x 11 inches
Margins:	.5 inch all sides
Orientation:	Tall (Portrait)
Other:	Create a border measuring 7 inches wide by 8 inches tall. Place the contents of the advertisement within this border.

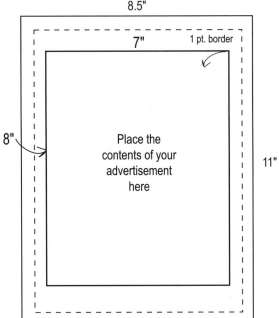

8.5"

7"

1 pt. border

8"

Place the
contents of your
advertisement
here

11"

Part 7:
Design a
Refrigerator Magnet

Approximate Completion Time: 1 hour

Design a Refrigerator Magnet

TASK AND PURPOSE:

To create and design a refrigerator magnet. To keep the name of Frillio's Pizza fresh in the minds of its customers, Mr. Frillio would like you to develop a business card size refrigerator magnet that will be distributed for free to all Frillio's Pizza customers. The objective of the magnet is to encourage customers to call Frillio's Pizza for takeout orders.

OPTIONAL MATERIALS SUGGESTED:

Peel and stick self-adhesive business card magnets.

GETTING TO KNOW WHAT YOU'RE DESIGNING:

People love sticking stuff to their refrigerators using magnets. Refrigerator magnets offer businesses a unique and creative marketing vehicle in which to convey their name, address, phone and fax numbers, and Web site address. Since refrigerator magnets tend to "stick" around for a long time, they make a great tool for restaurants to advertise right inside the family kitchen.

STRATEGIES AND DESIGN TIPS TO CONSIDER BEFORE CREATING YOUR REFRIGERATOR MAGNET:

1. Since space is limited, use only one typeface (font) in the design of the magnet.
2. Be sure to prominently display the phone number since it will be the most likely form of contact that customers will use.
3. Use the document planning sheet to sketch a thumbnail design of your refrigerator magnet on paper first.

CONTENT AND INFORMATION TO INCLUDE ON YOUR REFRIGERATOR MAGNET:

1. Include a headline at the top of the magnet that reads "Call Frillio's Pizza for Takeout or Delivery."

2. Include the Frillio's Pizza logo on your magnet.

3. Include the following contact information in the order shown:

    Phone Number: 1-888-FRILLIO
    Address: 111 Pepperoni Drive • Saucy, CA 92888
    Web Site: http://www.frilliospizza.com

    Note: When placing the contact information on the magnet, be sure that the phone number is the most visible item.

4. Include the Frillio's Pizza hours of operation, which are:

    Mon - Thurs 11 am - 9 pm
    Fri, Sat, & Sun 11 am - 10 pm

5. Add additional text or ONE graphic image that will help in getting customers to respond to the magnets. The suggested graphic image to use is a telephone.

6. Place your name, the document title, and "Part 7" on the magnet.

Save the document as: Part 7 Magnet

Optional Design-Defense Memo:
Type a letter of memorandum addressed to Joe Frillio explaining your design, placement, font selections, layout scheme, and choice of graphic image(s). Attach this memo to your final document.

REFRIGERATOR MAGNET PAGE SETUP INSTRUCTIONS:

# of pages: 1
Dimensions: 8.5 x 11 inches
Margins: 1 inch all sides
Orientation: Tall (Portrait)
Other: Create a border measuring 2 inches tall by 3.5 inches wide.
                    Place the contents of the magnet within this border.

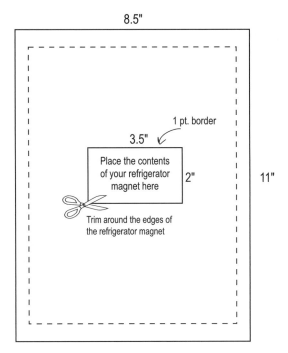

Optional: Stick the trimmed refrigerator magnet on a peel and stick self-adhesive business card magnet.

Part 8:
Design the Frillio's Pizza Takeout Menu Brochure

Approximate Completion Time: 3-4 hours

Design the Takeout Menu Brochure

TASK AND PURPOSE:

To create and design a three-panel brochure that will serve as the Frillio's Pizza takeout menu. All of the items and prices from the Frillio's Pizza menu will be used to create the takeout menu.

Note: You can save time by recalling the menu document created in Part 5 and copying and pasting the menu items and prices to help you create the takeout menu brochure.

OPTIONAL MATERIALS SUGGESTED:

Colored paper.

GETTING TO KNOW WHAT YOU'RE DESIGNING:

A brochure is a small booklet or pamphlet, often containing promotional material or product information. Brochures are usually folded into two, three, or four panels. Brochures are popular because they are relatively small when folded and take up less desk or file space. And, because brochures are two-sided documents, they can communicate a large amount of information in a relatively small amount of space.

In this case, the brochure will serve two purposes:
1. To advertise the Frillio's Pizza restaurant.
2. To provide customers with a takeout menu in a convenient size.

STRATEGIES AND DESIGN TIPS TO CONSIDER BEFORE CREATING YOUR TAKEOUT MENU BROCHURE:

1. Pay careful attention not to clutter the brochure. The design should have a consistent systematic flow that moves the reader from the outside front cover through the inside right panel.
2. Since you will be using the same items from the Frillio's Pizza menu previously created in Part 5, stick to the same theme and design scheme to establish consistency with the two menus.
3. Consider using a thin-line border on the inside three panels of the menu to "frame" the information contained on them.
4. To assist you in the layout and design of your takeout menu brochure, fold a blank sheet of paper, holding it the long way (landscape), into three equal columns. Label these columns as indicated in the page setup instructions and illustrations for this section. Sketch the brochure layout on this paper.

CONTENT AND INFORMATION TO INCLUDE BEFORE CREATING YOUR TAKEOUT MENU BROCHURE:

When folded, the brochure will be divided into three equally sized panels on each side. The purpose of each panel of the brochure, as well as the information to include on each panel, is given below.

Outside right panel of the brochure:
When folded, this is the part of the three-panel brochure that is seen first, and it is the most important. It should entice the reader to open and read the brochure.

Include the following on the outside right panel of the brochure:
1. A headline that reads "Frillio's Pizza Takeout Menu." This text should be placed near the top of the brochure and should be the largest text on the panel.

2. The Frillio's Pizza logo and the slogan "The best pizzeria in town."

3. The Frillio's Pizza phone number (1-888-FRILLIO) and the Web site address (www.frilliospizza.com).

4. Use a graphic image of an arrow pointing to the right. Near or on the arrow, place text that reads "See inside for our menu."

5. Add additional text or graphic images that will make the brochure look attractive and professional.

6. Place your name, the document title, and "Part 8" on the outside right panel of the takeout menu brochure.

Outside middle panel of the brochure:
When folded, this is the back panel of the brochure and is usually reserved for contact information.

Include the following on the outside middle panel of the brochure:
1. The Frillio's Pizza logo.

2. Include the following contact information:

    111 Pepperoni Drive, Saucy, CA 92888
    1-888-FRILLIO
    http://www.frilliospizza.com

    Note: The logo and contact information should be placed near the bottom of the panel.

3. Include the Frillio's Pizza hours of operation which are:

   Mon - Thurs 11 am - 9 pm
   Fri, Sat, & Sun 11 am - 10 pm

4. Add text that reads "We Deliver Every Day and Night of the Week."

5. In small print, add the text "All of our menu items are available for delivery with the exception of desserts and beverages."

6. Add additional text or graphic images that make the brochure look attractive and professional.

Outside left panel of the brochure:
When the front panel of the brochure is open, this is the panel that faces the reader. It is usually seen second. The back left panel is usually reserved for a message that gets the reader to open the brochure.

Include the following on the outside left panel of the brochure:
1. Include a message and/or graphic images that entice the reader to open and read the rest of the brochure. Example: "Our takeout menu brings the Frillio's Pizza spirit right to your own kitchen."

2. Create a cut-out style coupon on the inside right panel of the brochure that includes the following:
   • A dotted-line border to create the appearance of a cut-out coupon.
   • Text that reads "Free appetizer with your next takeout or delivery order when you present this coupon."
   • In fine print, include text that reads "Limit: one coupon per customer."
   • A small graphic image of an appetizer menu item on the interior of this coupon..

Inside three panels of the brochure:
When the brochure is open, the inside three panels face the reader. The inside panels are reserved for the body of the brochure. The information included can be separated into three columns, or spread across two or three of the inside panels.

Include the following on the inside three panels of the brochure:
1. Include all of the Frillio's Pizza menu items and prices on the inside three panels of the brochure. The menu items and prices can be found on pages 52 and 53. Be sure to pay attention to the placement of each category. Stay consistent with the design that you used to create the menu in Part 5.

2. Repeat the following text several times in the footer (bottom) area of the three inside panels: "Call Toll-free 1-888-FRILLIO."

3. Add additional text or graphic images that make the inside of the brochure look attractive and appeal to the senses of taste and smell.

Save the document as: Part 8 Takeout Menu

Optional Design-Defense Memo:
Type a letter of memorandum addressed to Joe Frillio explaining your design, placement, font selections, layout scheme, and choice of graphic image(s). Attach this memo to your final document.

TAKEOUT MENU BROCHURE PAGE SETUP INSTRUCTIONS:

# of pages: 2
Dimensions: 11 x 8.5 inches
Margins: .25 inches all sides
Orientation: Wide (Landscape)
Other: Use page or column guides to divide both sides of the brochure into three equal panels. Leave a .5 inch gutter space between each column to allow for folding. Do not place any contents inside the .5" gutter space on either side of the menu (see the page setup illustration below for more help).
Printing Note: Print the takeout menu back-to-back (double-sided) on your printer or print both sheets separately and staple them together.

Page 1 - Outside of takeout menu brochure

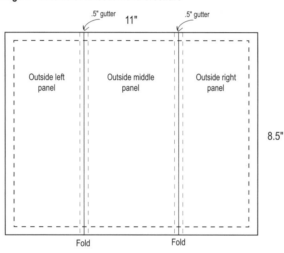

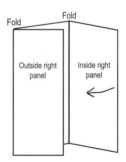

When folded, the finished takeout menu brochure should look like this

Page 2 - Inside of takeout menu brochure

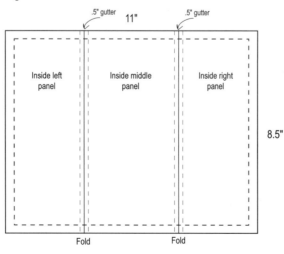

Part 9: Create a Bumper Sticker

Approximate Completion Time: 1 hour

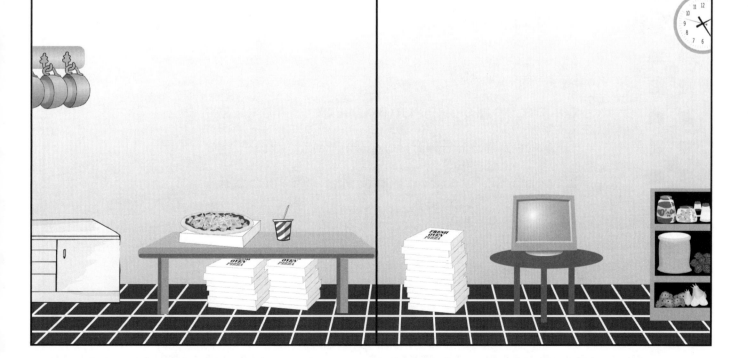

Create a Bumper Sticker

TASK AND PURPOSE:

To create and design a bumper sticker that will be used as a promotional document to advertise Frillio's Pizza. The bumper sticker will be given to customers free of charge.

OPTIONAL MATERIALS SUGGESTED:

Full sheet laser or ink-jet compatible printer labels.

GETTING TO KNOW WHAT YOU'RE DESIGNING:

A bumper sticker is a sticker bearing a printed message for display on a vehicle's bumper. With so many cars on the road today, bumper stickers are a highly visible marketing tool for businesses. Due to limited driver visibility, bumper stickers are reserved for conveying only one message to the reader.

STRATEGIES AND DESIGN TIPS TO CONSIDER BEFORE CREATING YOUR BUMPER STICKER:

1. Use a poster or block style typeface (font) to maximize the visibility of the message.
2. Since space is limited, use only one graphic on your bumper sticker.
3. Leave plenty of white space to maximize the readability of your bumper sticker.
4. When designing your bumper sticker, work your layout scheme in a horizontal fashion from left to right.
5. Use the document planning sheet to sketch a thumbnail design of your bumper sticker on paper first.

CONTENT AND INFORMATION TO INCLUDE ON THE BUMPER STICKER:

1. A large headline that prominently displays the text "Frillio's Pizza" on it.

2. A subheading that displays the Frillio's Pizza slogan "The best pizzeria in town."

3. The Frillio's Pizza logo.

4. A large, easy-to-read typeface showing Frillio's Pizza's phone number "1-888-FRILLIO."

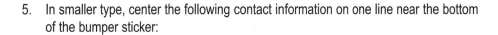

5. In smaller type, center the following contact information on one line near the bottom of the bumper sticker:

    111 Pepperoni Drive, Saucy, CA 92888 • http://www.frilliospizza.com

6. Add additional text OR one graphic image that you feel will help to get the bumper stickers noticed by drivers and onlookers. Use caution: Your space is very limited! Do not clutter the bumper sticker so much that it becomes difficult to read.

7. Place your name, the document title, and "Part 9" on the bumper sticker.

Save the document as: Part 9 Bumper Sticker

Optional Design-Defense Memo:
Type a letter of memorandum addressed to Joe Frillio explaining your design, placement, font selections, layout scheme, and choice of graphic image(s). Attach this memo to your final document.

BUMPER STICKER PAGE SETUP INSTRUCTIONS:

# of pages: 1
Dimensions: 11 x 8.5 inches
Margins: .25 inches all sides
Orientation: Wide (Landscape)
Other: Create a border measuring 3 inches tall by 10.5 inches wide.
     Place the contents of the bumper sticker within this border.
     Use scissors to trim around the edges of the bumper sticker.

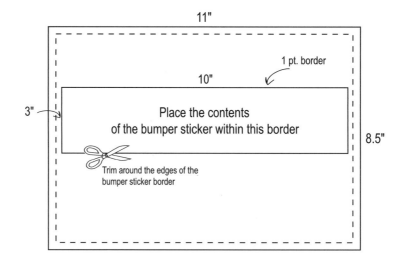

11"

1 pt. border

10"

3"

Place the contents
of the bumper sticker within this border

8.5"

Trim around the edges of the
bumper sticker border

Part 10: Create an Hours of Operation Sign

Approximate Completion Time: 1 hour

Create an Hours
of Operation Sign

TASK AND PURPOSE:

To create and design an "Hours of Operation" sign that will be placed in a window or door to let customers know when Frillio's Pizza is open for business.

GETTING TO KNOW WHAT YOU'RE DESIGNING:

Just about every retail establishment posts its hours of operation in a highly-visible area. Hours of operation signs let customers know when they can enter an establishment.

STRATEGIES AND DESIGN TIPS TO CONSIDER BEFORE CREATING YOUR HOURS OF OPERATION SIGN:

1. Experiment with a variety of borders to frame in the content of your hours of operation sign.
2. Use a poster or block style typeface (font) to maximize the visibility of the sign.
3. With the exception of the Frillio's Pizza logo, this is a text-only document. There is no reason to include any additional graphic images.
4. Use a type size that allows the sign to be read easily from a distance.
5. Use the document planning sheet to sketch a thumbnail design of your hours of operation on paper first.

CONTENT AND INFORMATION TO INCLUDE ON YOUR HOURS OF OPERATION SIGN:

1. A centered headline placed at the top of the sign that reads "Frillio's Pizza – Hours Open."

2. The Frillio's Pizza logo.

3. List the hours of operation, using a format similar to the one shown below (be sure that the type is large enough to read from a distance):

Monday	11 am – 9 pm
Tuesday	11 am – 9 pm
Wednesday	11 am – 9 pm
Thursday	11 am – 9 pm
Friday	11 am – 10 pm
Saturday	11 am – 10 pm
Sunday	11 am – 10 pm

4. A page border to frame the information.

5. Place your name, the document title, and "Part 10" on the hours of operation sign.

Save the document as: Part 10 Hours of Operation

Optional Design-Defense Memo:
Type a letter of memorandum addressed to Joe Frillio explaining your design, placement, font selections, layout scheme, and choice of graphic image(s). Attach this memo to your final document.

HOURS OF OPERATION SIGN PAGE SETUP INSTRUCTIONS:

# of pages: 1
Dimensions: 8.5 x 11 inches
Margins: .5 inches all sides
Orientation: Tall (Portrait)
Other: Create a border measuring 7 inches wide by 10 inches tall. Place the contents of the hours of operation sign within this border.

8.5"

7"

Place the contents of the hours of operation sign within this border

10" 11"

Part 11:
Create a "Pizza Club" Promotional Punch Card

Approximate Completion Time: 1 - 2 hours

PROMOTIONAL
PUNCH CARDS

Frillio's

Create a "Pizza Club" Promotional Punch Card

TASK AND PURPOSE:

To create a promotional punch card to encourage customers to return to Frillio's Pizza and to thank customers for their loyalty. The promotion is called the "Pizza Club" and here's how it works:

The punch card will contain five small symbols (to be selected by you) printed on it. Every Frillio's Pizza customer will be given one "Pizza Club" punch card. Each time a customer dines at Frillio's Pizza, or orders takeout, one of the symbols on the punch card will be hole-punched. When a customer's "Pizza Club" card has all five symbols punched out, he or she earns one free large pizza or another menu item of equal or lesser value.

OPTIONAL MATERIALS SUGGESTED:

Cardstock paper.

GETTING TO KNOW WHAT YOU'RE DESIGNING:

Businesses often use special promotions to encourage repeat business and to build customer loyalty. To illustrate this concept, think of an airline company. Airlines often offer its passengers "frequent flyer miles." The passenger receives additional free miles each time he or she flies with the same airline company. Similarly, a retail store may present customers with a "10% off card" to promote a special sales event.

In this case, the promotional document you will create is a "Pizza Club Card" to encourage customers to return to Frillio's Pizza.

STRATEGIES AND DESIGN TIPS TO CONSIDER BEFORE CREATING YOUR PIZZA CLUB PROMOTIONAL PUNCH CARD:

1. Use a lottery ticket as a guide to help you lay out your punch card.
2. To get an idea about what size to make the item to be punched on the pizza club card, use a hole puncher and punch several holes out on a sheet of paper.
3. Be sure the item you select to be "punched" displays large enough to be seen and punched.
4. Consider framing in the items to be punched with a bordered box.
5. Use the document planning sheet to sketch a thumbnail design of your promotional punch card on paper first.

CONTENT AND INFORMATION TO INCLUDE ON YOUR PIZZA CLUB PROMOTIONAL PUNCH CARD:

1. Select a graphic image that will represent the symbol that will be punched on the card. This graphic image will be repeated five times on the promotional punch cards. Possibilities include a slice of pizza, a pizza pan, a pizza cutter and so on. Arrange these items next to each other horizontally near the bottom of the Pizza Club Card. The distance between each image should be equal.

2. Place a headline on the top center of the card that reads "Pizza Club Card."

3. Include the Frillio's Pizza logo.

4. Place the following text just below the headline area:

   "Get five (the symbol you selected) punched and earn one FREE large pizza or another menu item of equal or lesser value."

5. Using a smaller type size than you did in step 4 above, include the following text just below the area where you placed the text from step 4 above:

   "**Here's How The Pizza Club Card Works:** Each time you dine in, takeout, or order delivery, just present this card to any employee and get one (the symbol you selected) punched. When all five (your symbol) are punched, return your card for a free large pizza or another menu item of equal or lesser value."

6. Add additional text and/or graphic images you feel will make the promotional punch card look creative and professional. Use caution: Space is limited. You already have five graphic images that represent the symbols to be punched.

7. Place your name, the document title, and "Part 11" on the reverse side of your promotional punch card.

Save the document as: Part 11 Punch Card

Optional Design-Defense Memo:
Type a letter of memorandum addressed to Joe Frillio explaining your design, placement, font selections, layout scheme, and choice of graphic image(s). Attach this memo to your final document.

PIZZA CLUB PROMOTIONAL PUNCH CARD PAGE SETUP INSTRUCTIONS:

# of pages: 1
Dimensions: 8.5 x 11 inches
Margins: 1 inch all sides
Orientation: Tall (Portrait)
Other: Create a border measuring 5 inches wide by 4 inches tall. Place the contents of the punch card within this border. Use scissors to trim around the edges of the punch card border.

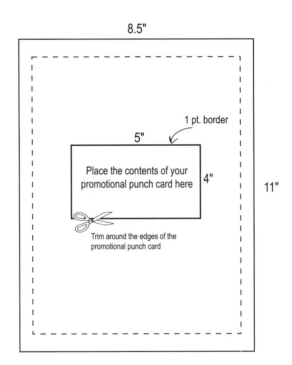

8.5"

1 pt. border

5"

Place the contents of your
promotional punch card here

4"

11"

Trim around the edges of the
promotional punch card

Part 12:
Create a
Cup Coaster

Approximate Completion Time: 1 hour

Create a Cup Coaster

TASK AND PURPOSE:

To create a cup coaster that will be placed underneath customer's beverages.

OPTIONAL MATERIALS SUGGESTED:

Cardstock paper.

GETTING TO KNOW WHAT YOU'RE DESIGNING:

Cup coasters help protect tables from being scratched. They also offer an effective way to "brand" the name of a food establishment into the minds of its customers. Cup coasters also add a small touch of personalization to the atmosphere of a food establishment.

STRATEGIES AND DESIGN TIPS TO CONSIDER BEFORE CREATING YOUR CUP COASTER:

1. Experiment with various round borders to help frame in the contents of your coaster.
2. Because the coasters are round, consider using arched text.
3. Consider using a background pattern to add visual appeal to your cup coaster.
4. Use the document planning sheet to sketch a thumbnail design of your cup coaster on paper first.

CONTENT AND INFORMATION TO INCLUDE ON YOUR CUP COASTER:

1. Create a message that thanks customers for eating at Frillio's Pizza.

2. Include the Frillio's Pizza logo.

3. Add additional text or graphic images that will make the cup coasters look creative and professional.

4. Write your name, the document title, and "Part 12" on the back of the cup coaster.

Save the document as: Part 12 Cup Coaster

Optional Design-Defense Memo:
Type a letter of memorandum addressed to Joe Frillio explaining your design, placement, font selections, layout scheme, and choice of graphic image(s). Attach this memo to your final document.

CUP COASTER PAGE SETUP INSTRUCTIONS:

# of pages: 1
Dimensions: 8.5 x 11 inches
Margins: 1 inch on all sides
Orientation: Tall (Portrait)
Other: Create a perfect circle border measuring 5 inches in diameter. Place the contents of the cup coaster within this border. Use scissors to trim around the edges of the cup coaster border.

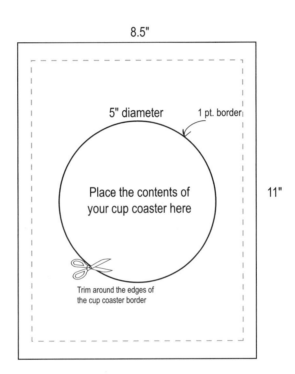

8.5"

5" diameter   1 pt. border

Place the contents of
your cup coaster here

11"

Trim around the edges of
the cup coaster border

Part 13:
Create a
Gift Certificate

Approximate Completion Time: 1.5 hours

Create a Gift Certificate

TASK AND PURPOSE:

To create a gift certificate for Frillio's Pizza.

OPTIONAL MATERIALS SUGGESTED:

Colored paper.

GETTING TO KNOW WHAT YOU'RE DESIGNING:

A gift certificate is usually presented as a gift from one person to another and entitles the recipient to select products of a specific cash value at a business establishment. Gift certificates are usually printed on heavy bond paper so they will stand the test of time. Gift certificates help businesses generate sales and bring in new customers (the recipient(s)). Since they make great gifts, gift certificates are very popular around the holiday season.

STRATEGIES AND DESIGN TIPS TO CONSIDER BEFORE CREATING YOUR GIFT CERTIFICATE:

1. Consider using a double-line thin border to add a touch of professionalism to the gift certificate.
2. For the headline of the gift certificate, experiment with the use of a script style typeface (font). Script style fonts give the impression that the words were actually hand-drawn on the document.
3. Limit the use of graphics to one (not including the logo). Any more will make the gift certificate appear cluttered.
4. Use the document planning sheet to sketch a thumbnail design of your gift certificate on paper first.

CONTENT AND INFORMATION TO INCLUDE ON YOUR GIFT CERTIFICATES:

1. On the top center, place the text "Gift Certificate." This text should be the largest element on the gift certificate.

2. Include the Frillio's Pizza logo and the following contact information on the gift certificate:

Address:	111 Pepperoni Drive, Saucy, CA 92888
Phone Number:	1-888-FRILLIO
Web Site Address:	http://www.frilliospizza.com

3. Include the following text: "Enjoy great tasting pizza, sandwiches, Italian dishes, and appetizers—all in a fun and friendly atmosphere."

4. Create an area that allows for the following information to be filled in:

    "To," "From," "Date," and "Amount"

5. Add additional text or graphic images you feel will make the gift certificates look creative, professional, and welcoming to the recipient (the person who will receive the gift certificate).

6. Place your name, the document title, and "Part 13" on the back of the gift certificate.

Save the document as: Part 13 Gift Certificate

Optional Design-Defense Memo:
Type a letter of memorandum addressed to Joe Frillio explaining your design, placement, font selections, layout scheme, and choice of graphic image(s). Attach this memo to your final document.

GIFT CERTIFICATE PAGE SETUP INSTRUCTIONS:

# of pages: 1
Dimensions: 8.5 x 11 inches
Margins: .5 inches on all sides
Orientation: Tall (Portrait)
Other: Create a border measuring 7.5 inches wide by 3.375 inches tall. Place the contents of the gift certificate within this border.

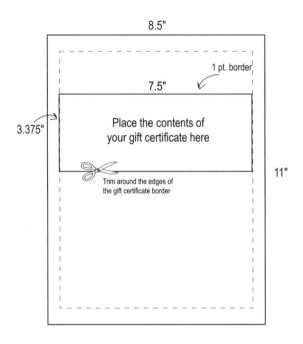

Part 14:
Frillio's Pizza T-shirt
Design on a Flyer

Approximate Completion Time: 2 hours

Frillio's Pizza T-shirt Design on a Flyer

TASK AND PURPOSE:

This part involves two separate steps that will be combined into one document. Step one is to create a design for Frillio's Pizza T-shirts. Step two is to add the T-shirt design to a flyer announcing a weekly free T-shirt giveaway. Frillio's Pizza will hold a weekly raffle in which one customer per week will win a free Frillio's Pizza T-shirt. The T-shirts are a way of saying "thank you" to customers for dining at Frillio's Pizza. The T-shirt will also help to promote the Frillio's Pizza establishment.

GETTING TO KNOW WHAT YOU'RE DESIGNING:

T-shirt designs take on many forms, from simple text to detailed graphics. T-shirts imprinted with an organization's logo offer a walking form of free advertising.

STRATEGIES AND DESIGN TIPS TO CONSIDER BEFORE CREATING YOUR T-SHIRT:

1. Be sure that the message on the T-shirt is in a block style typeface (font) to make it easy to read.
2. Make the graphic of your T-shirt design large enough to see when placed on the flyer.
3. Use the document planning sheet to sketch a thumbnail design of your T-shirt design and flyer on paper first.

CONTENT AND INFORMATION TO INCLUDE ON YOUR T-SHIRT DESIGN FLYER:
Note: There are two separate steps to complete this part of the simulation. However, you will combine these steps to produce only one document.

Step 1: Create the Frillio's Pizza T-shirt design

To create the Frillio's Pizza T-shirt design, place the following inside a graphic image of a T-shirt (available at www.frilliospizza.com):

- A catchy headline that conveys a message about the food and service at Frillio's Pizza
- The Frillio's Pizza logo and slogan "The best pizzeria in town"
- The phone number "1-888-FRILLIO"

Use your imagination and creativity to make the T-shirt design desirable for customers to wear.

**Step 2: Create a Flyer to Announce the Frillio's Pizza Free T-shirt
Giveaway**

Include the following on the flyer:

1. Create a "catchy" headline for the flyer to announce the free T-shirt giveaway.

2. Include the following text below the headline:

    "Win a free Frillio's Pizza T-shirt by entering our weekly drawing. To enter, please fill out an entry form located on the front cashier's counter."

3. Add the graphic image of the T-shirt design you created in step 1 to the flyer. The graphic of the T-shirt design should be prominently displayed on the flyer.

4. Include the following text near the bottom of the T-shirt flyer:

    "One size fits all. T-shirt drawing is held every Friday night. If you are not present during the drawing, we will contact you by phone or e-mail."

5. Add additional text and/or graphic images to make the flyer appealing and professional looking.

6. Place your name, the document title, and "Part 14" on the T-shirt design flyer.

Save the document as: Part 14 T-shirt Flyer

Optional Design-Defense Memo:
Type a letter of memorandum addressed to Joe Frillio explaining your design, placement, font selections, layout scheme, and choice of graphic image(s). Attach this memo to your final document.

T-SHIRT DESIGN ON A FLYER PAGE SETUP INSTRUCTIONS:

# of pages: 1
Dimensions: 8.5 x 11 inches
Margins: .5 inches on all sides
Orientation: Tall (Portrait)
Other: Place the T-shirt design inside a graphic image of a T-shirt on the flyer.

Your T-shirt design should be placed on a graphic image of a T-shirt similar to the one shown here. Then, place this graphic on your flyer.

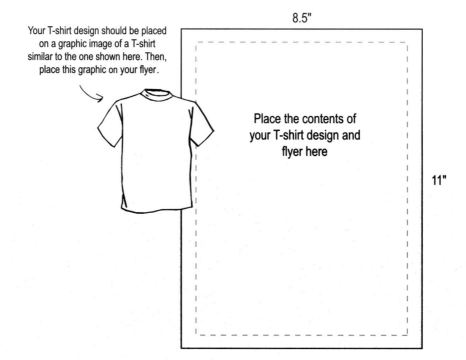

8.5"

Place the contents of your T-shirt design and flyer here

11"

Bonus #1: Create a Poster

Approximate Completion Time: 2 hours

Create a Poster

TASK AND PURPOSE:

To create a poster that will be placed in high-traffic areas on the walls inside of Frillio's Pizza.

The purpose of the poster is to:

1. Remind customers of the friendly atmosphere they will find at Frillio's Pizza.
2. Showcase the most popular menu items offered.
3. Convey the good spirit customers will find while dining at the restaurant.

OPTIONAL MATERIALS SUGGESTED:

Colored paper.

GETTING TO KNOW WHAT YOU'RE DESIGNING:

Posters come in a variety of shapes, sizes, and colors. They can be used to announce new movies, plays, special sales events, and many other things. A poster usually contains a large headline in conjunction with a coordinating graphic image or photo.

STRATEGIES AND DESIGN TIPS TO CONSIDER BEFORE CREATING YOUR POSTER:

1. An effective poster should be attractive, well-organized and self-explanatory with the text and graphics linked to the audience at hand.
2. The headline should be the largest element of the poster. It should be readable from at least five feet away. Consider using a block style typeface (font) for the headline.
3. Decide on the major sections of information that will be included in the poster to support your main point; organize these into a logical flow.
4. Select graphic images that are closely tied to your major points. There should be a clear reason for each image, and each image should be tied to the text.
5. Avoid cluttering the poster with too many images—if the connection between an image and one of your main points is not immediately clear, don't include it just for the sake of visual appeal.
6. Use the document planning sheet to sketch a thumbnail design of your poster on paper first.

CONTENT AND INFORMATION TO INCLUDE ON YOUR POSTER:

1. The poster's headline should read:

   "At Frillio's Pizza, We Take Pride in Our Friendly Service and Quality Food."

2. Include the Frillio's Pizza logo and be sure it is prominently displayed near the top of the poster.

3. Include a bulleted list within a square border that includes the following menu items:

    • Fresh Oven-baked Pizza
    • Frillio's Special Sandwich
    • Great Appetizers
    • Delicious Italian Dishes

    Create a heading for this bulleted list and include it just above or inside the square border.

4. Place the following text, in small print, just below or inside the square border containing the above bulleted list:

    "Our menu items contain no food additives or preservatives."

5. Add additional text or graphic images to make the poster an attractive, eye-catching document.

6. Place your name, the document title, and "Bonus #1" on the poster.

Save the document as: Bonus 1 Poster

Optional Design-Defense Memo:
Type a letter of memorandum addressed to Joe Frillio explaining your design, placement, font selections, layout scheme, and choice of graphic image(s). Attach this memo to your final document.

POSTER PAGE SETUP INSTRUCTIONS:

# of pages:	1
Dimensions:	8.5 x 11 inches
Margins:	.25 inches on all sides
Orientation:	Tall (Portrait)
Other:	Create a border measuring 8 inches wide by 10.5 inches tall. Place the contents of the poster within this border.

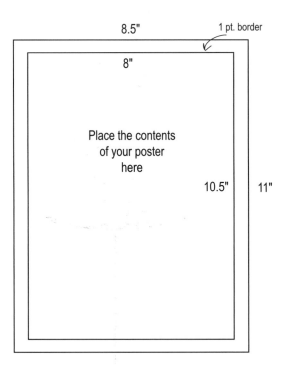

Note: Although you will be printing your poster on an 8.5 x 11 inch sheet of paper, Joe Frillio will be having it blown up to print on 17 x 22 inch poster-size paper.

Bonus #2:
Create a T-shirt
Raffle Entry Form

Approximate Completion Time: 1 - 1.5 hours

Create a T-shirt Raffle
Entry Form

TASK AND PURPOSE:

To create a T-shirt raffle entry form. The form will be filled out by customers of Frillio's Pizza who choose to enter the weekly T-shirt giveaway (as explained in Part 14).

OPTIONAL MATERIALS SUGGESTED:

Cardstock paper.

GETTING TO KNOW WHAT YOU'RE DESIGNING:

Forms are a part of every business—from job and college applications, to loans and surveys. The purpose of a form is simple—to collect information.

STRATEGIES AND DESIGN TIPS TO CONSIDER BEFORE CREATING YOUR RAFFLE ENTRY FORM:

1. Be sure to allow plenty of space between the lines.
2. Be sure each line or box of information is wide enough for the customer to fit the requested information.
3. Include the text "print neatly" to make the information easy to read.
4. Use the same typeface (font) throughout the form. There is no need to get fancy when designing a form. The information you are requesting should be presented to the reader in a clear and concise manner.
5. Be sure to include instructions on what to do with the form once it is filled in completely.
6. Use the document planning sheet to sketch a thumbnail design of your T-shirt raffle entry form on paper first.

CONTENT AND INFORMATION TO INCLUDE ON YOUR T-SHIRT RAFFLE ENTRY FORM:

1. At the top of the form, include the text "Win a Free Frillio's Pizza T-shirt."

2. Next to the text at the top of the form, include a small graphic image of the T-shirt and its design that you created in Part 14.

3. On the next line, include the following text:

   "Just fill out and drop this form in the box labeled *T-shirt Drawing* located on the cashier's counter. You may enter as many times as you'd like."

3. Include the text "Please print neatly" just above the first line of entry on the form.

4. Request that the customer fill out the lines of entry shown below. Add thin straight lines next to or above each item of requested information.

   > First Name
   > Last Name
   > Address
   > City, State, Zip
   > Phone
   > *E-mail Address:
   > *Your e-mail address will never be rented or sold

5. Add a line of text that reads "Please tell us how we're doing..."
   Just beneath this text, create small check-off boxes next to the following words as shown below:

   ☐ Excellent   ☐ Good   ☐ Average ☐ Could be better

6. Add a section for customers to write in any additional comments they would like to add to the form.

7. Arrange the requested information neatly on the card.

8. In small print, include the following text near the bottom of the form:

   "One size fits all. T-shirt drawing is held every Friday evening. You do not have to be present to win. No purchase required to enter. If you are a winner, we will contact you by phone or e-mail."

9. Write your name, the document title, and "Bonus #2" on the reverse side of the raffle entry form.

Save the document as: Bonus 2 Raffle Form

Optional Design-Defense Memo:
Type a letter of memorandum addressed to Joe Frillio explaining your design, placement, font selections, layout scheme, and choice of graphic image(s). Attach this memo to your final document.

T-SHIRT RAFFLE ENTRY FORM PAGE SETUP INSTRUCTIONS:

# of pages: 1
Dimensions: 8.5 x 11 inches
Margins: .5 inches on all sides
Orientation: Tall (Portrait)
Other: Create a border measuring 6 inches wide by 4 inches tall. Place the contents of the form within this border.

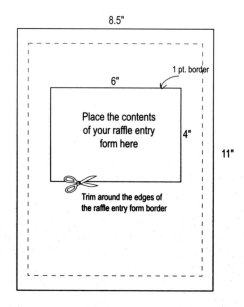

Bonus #3:
Create an Employment Application Form

Approximate Completion Time: 1 - 1.5 hours

EMPLOYMENT
APPLICATION
FORM

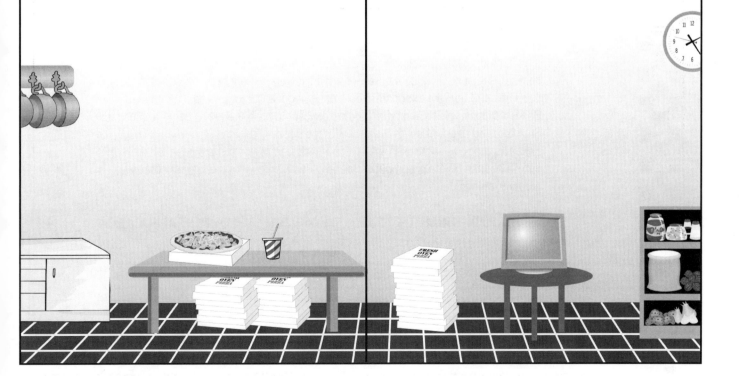

Create an Employment Application Form

TASK AND PURPOSE:

To create and design a Frillio's Pizza employment application form. The form will be used to gather information about prospective Frillio's Pizza employees. The employment application form will be used to hire dishwashers, chefs, bus boys/girls, hostesses, cashier clerks, and wait staff.

GETTING TO KNOW WHAT YOU'RE DESIGNING:

Employment application forms (commonly referred to as "job applications"), are a standard document used by practically every type of business in existence. They allow the prospective employer a means in which to gather important information and data about the job applicant. While the type of information requested on job applications may vary slightly from business to business, most are relatively the same. A typical job application form will ask the applicant to provide personal data, such as name and address, and to list education and work experience.

STRATEGIES AND DESIGN TIPS TO CONSIDER BEFORE CREATING YOUR EMPLOYMENT APPLICATION FORM:

1.   Job application forms are not the place to add fancy design elements or graphic images. The document should be clean, professional, and easy to read.
2.   Use either boxes or straight lines for the areas of information that need to be filled out.
3.   If warranted, create a table of rows and columns when creating areas that ask the applicant to list items such as present and past work experience and education.
4.   Use lines and borders to separate different categories of requested information.
5.   Be sure to leave plenty of space for the applicant to fill in the areas being requested.
6.   Stick to using one font throughout the job application's design.
7.   Try using graph paper to plan the layout and design of your employment application form. The lines on the graph paper will assist you in keeping the different areas properly aligned.

CONTENT AND INFORMATION TO INCLUDE ON YOUR EMPLOYMENT APPLICATION FORM:

1.   Place the Frillio's Pizza logo in the top area of the employment application form.

2. Place the following text in the top center of the job application form:

   "Frillio's Pizza Employment Application Form"

3. Using a small type size, add the following text just below the text you placed from step 2 above:

   "Please give your completed application to any manager. Upon reviewing your application, someone will contact you for an interview if a position becomes available."

4. Use a border to frame the requested areas of information shown in step 5.

5. Using straight lines or rectangular boxes, create the areas of information shown below for applicants to complete the employment application form. Be sure to arrange and organize the information areas neatly on your employment application form.

Information to include on the employment application form ▼

PERSONAL INFORMATION
Name
Address
City
State
Zip Code
Phone Number
E-mail Address

JOB INTERESTS
Position Desired
Are you seeking part-time or full-time employment? Part-time Full-Time
Desired starting hourly wage
Have you ever worked in a restaurant before? Yes or No
If yes, what position(s) did you hold?

OTHER
Have you ever been convicted of a misdemeanor or felony? Yes or No
If yes, please explain
Are you 18 years of age or older? Yes or No
Are you a U.S. citizen or legally authorized to work in the United States? Yes or No
Do you hold a valid driver's license? Yes or No

AVAILABILITY
Days and times you are available to work (please circle all that apply):
    Monday Day/Eve, Tuesday Day/Eve, Wednesday Day/Eve,
    Thursday Day/Eve, Friday Day/Eve, Saturday Day/Eve, Sunday Day/Eve

REFERENCES
Please list the names and phone numbers of three references.

EDUCATION
School Most Recently Attended/Attending
Highest Level Degree Earned
Year of Graduation

WORK EXPERIENCE *(Include room for the applicant to list his or her last three employers)*
Position Held
Company
Employed from _____ to _____
Reason for Leaving

6. Using a small type size, add the following text to the bottom center of the job application form:

    "Frillio's Pizza does not discriminate on the basis of age, sex, color, race, religion, national origin, or disability in accordance with applicable laws and regulations."

7. Write your name on the "Name" line on the employment application form.

Save the document as: Bonus 3 Employment Form

Optional Design-Defense Memo:
Type a letter of memorandum addressed to Joe Frillio explaining your design, placement, font selections, layout scheme, and choice of graphic image(s). Attach this memo to your final document.

EMPLOYMENT APPLICATION FORM PAGE SETUP INSTRUCTIONS:

# of pages:	1
Dimensions:	8.5 x 11 inches
Margins:	.5 inches on all sides
Orientation:	Tall (Portrait)

8.5"

Place the contents of your employment application form here

11"

Conclusion:
Download the
"Job Complete"
Title Page

Download the "Job Complete" Title Page

CONGRATULATIONS!

You have successfully completed the Frillio's Pizza Desktop Publishing Simulation.

Using the documents you have just produced, Joe Frillio can now declare his restaurant, Frillio's Pizza, officially "open."

Your final task is to visit the Frillio's Pizza Web site at *www.frilliospizza.com* to download and print the "Job Complete" Title Page. You can find the form and instructions on how to download it under the section labeled "downloads" on the Web site.

Once you have downloaded and printed the form, fill out the required areas, attach all of the documents you have created, and submit it to your teacher for grading.

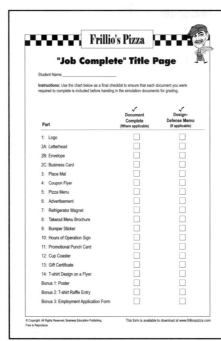

Your final task is to download, print, and fill out the "Job Complete" Title Page from the Frillio's Pizza Web site at *www.frilliospizza.com*.

If you do not have Internet access, you can obtain a copy of the "Job Complete" Title Page from your teacher.